From Ashes
to Fire

From Ashes to Fire

**Services of Worship
for the Seasons of Lent and Easter
with Introduction and Commentary**

Supplemental Worship Resources 8

ABINGDON
Nashville
1979

FROM ASHES TO FIRE

Copyright © 1979 by Abingdon

ISBN 0-687-136342

MANUFACTURED BY THE PARTHENON PRESS AT
NASHVILLE, TENNESSEE, UNITED STATES OF AMERICA

Contents

Preface

From Ashes to Fire is the eighth in the Supplemental Worship Resources series (SWR)—originally called the Alternate Rituals series—developed and sponsored by the Section on Worship of the Board of Discipleship of The United Methodist Church.

When The United Methodist Church was formed in 1968, *The Book of Discipline* provided (Par. 1388) that

the hymnals of The United Methodist Church are the hymnals of The Evangelical United Brethren Church and *The Methodist Hymnal* [later retitled *The Book of Hymns*]; the Ritual of the Church is that contained in the *Book of Ritual* of The Evangelical United Brethren Church, 1959, and *The Book of Worship for Church and Home* of The Methodist Church.

It quickly became apparent, however, that there was a need for supplemental worship resources which, while not taking the place of these official resources, would provide alternatives that more fully reflect developments in the

7

contemporary ecumenical church. The General Conference of 1970 authorized the Commission on Worship to begin work in this area, and the General Conferences of 1972 and 1976 authorized the Board of Discipleship "to develop standards and resources for the conduct of public worship in the churches" (1976 *Book of Discipline,* Par. 1316.2). The resulting series of publications began with *The Sacrament of the Lord's Supper: An Alternate Text 1972* (SWR 1), which was published both in a Text Edition and later (1975) in a Music Edition. Intensive work during the next four years led to the publication in 1976 of *A Service of Baptism, Confirmation, and Renewal: An Alternate Text 1976* (SWR 2), *Word and Table: A Basic Pattern of Sunday Worship for United Methodists* (SWR 3), and *Ritual in a New Day: An Invitation* (SWR 4). In 1973 the process was begun toward the publication of *A Service of Christian Marriage* (SWR 5) and *A Service of Death and Resurrection* (SWR 7). In 1977 the process was begun toward the publication of *Seasons of the Gospel: Resources for the Christian Year* (SWR 6) and the present volume. Further publications in this series are in preparation and will appear soon.

From Ashes to Fire builds upon the understanding of Sunday worship presented in *Word and Table* and the comprehensive understanding of the Christian year presented in *Seasons of the Gospel,* and the reader can profitably read both these other volumes for the further understanding of the present volume.

Like the other publications in this series, *From Ashes to Fire* represents the corporate work of the writers and consultants, and of the Section on Worship acting as an editorial committee. This committee determined the original specifications and carefully examined and edited the manuscript before approving it for publication.

Professor Don E. Saliers of Emory University was the writer of the manuscript. From time to time during the writing of the manuscript he held consultations with Professor James F. White of Perkins School of Theology at Southern Methodist University and Dr. Hoyt L. Hickman of the Section on Worship staff. These three persons had formed the task force which wrote *Word and Table* and *Seasons of the Gospel,* and their continuing consultation on this volume has helped insure its continuity of approach to that of the other two volumes. Rabbi Solomon Bernards, Director of the Department of Interreligious Cooperation of the Anti-Defamation League of B'Nai B'Rith, supplied suggestions and texts for the Seder published in chapter 12. He, Professor Lawrence A. Hoffman of Hebrew Union College Jewish Institute of Religion, and Rabbi Leon Klenicki, Director of the Department of Jewish-Catholic Relations of the Anti-Defamation League, consulted with Dr. Saliers regarding the implications of Holy Week liturgies for Jewish-Christian relations. Father Michael Marx of Saint John's Abbey, Collegeville, Minnesota, read through the manuscript and made helpful suggestions. General manuscript preparation was done by Hoyt L. Hickman, Everland Robinson, and Theresa Santillán in the office of the Section on Worship.

The members and staff of the Section on Worship, listed below, wish to thank the persons named above and many others who have shared with us ideas and resources for the seasons of Lent and Easter. Reactions to this volume, comments or suggestions, and any materials that have been created or discovered are welcomed by the Section on Worship, P. O. Box 840, Nashville, Tennessee 37202. We commend this volume to the use of local churches in the hope that it will be useful in the worship of God and the proclamation of the gospel of Jesus Christ.

FROM ASHES TO FIRE

Bishop Robert E. Goodrich, Jr.
Chairperson, Section on Worship

James F. White
Chairperson, Editorial Committee

Paul F. Abel
Phyllis Close
Edward L. Duncan
Judy Gilreath
Kay Hereford
Judith Kelsey-Powell

Marilynn Mabee
L. Doyle Masters
William B. McClain
Louise H. Shown
Carlton R. Young

Philip E. Baker, Ex Officio
representing the Fellowship of United Methodist Musicians

Elise M. Shoemaker, Ex Officio
representing the United Methodist Society for Worship

Roberto Escamilla, Associate General Secretary
Hoyt L. Hickman, Assistant General Secretary
Thom C. Jones, Staff

I.

Proclaiming
the Paschal Mystery:
An Introduction
to the Seasons
of Lent and Easter

At the heart of the Christian faith is our participation in the life, suffering, death, resurrection, and ascension of Jesus Christ as Lord. We proclaim that "the Word became flesh and dwelt among us" (John 1:14). Jesus Christ was born into human history in the fullness of time for our salvation. In time he lived and suffered, and was put to death; but God "raised him from the dead and made him sit at his right hand . . . , and has put all things under his feet and has made him the head over all things for the church, which is his body, the fulness of him who fills all in all" (Ephesians 1:20, 22-23 RSV). Through the death and resurrection of Jesus Christ we are delivered from sin and death, and by the Holy Spirit are born into eternal life wih God. This we confess; this we must renew continually in our lives.

What is this "Paschal Mystery" which is the very heart of the Christian gospel and of all our worship and life? Most United Methodists are probably unfamiliar with the expression. It comes from the word *pascha* (suffer) in the ancient Greek, Latin, and Syriac, and it came into English during the medieval period. We are more familiar with the term "passover," which translates the term *pasch* in various English versions of the Bible and some hymn texts. "Passover" is a celebration of the ancient Hebrew agricultural spring feast and of the historic rescue and deliverance from bondage in Egypt which occurred at that time of the year. The paschal lamb which was sacrificed to God in memory of that night of deliverance from death becomes a central symbol of redemption. It appears in the New Testament, especially in John's Gospel and in the writings of St. Paul. "Christ our passover is sacrificed for us: Therefore let us keep the feast" (I Corinthians 5:7-8).

When we speak of the Paschal Mystery, then, we refer to the whole range of meanings associated with the saving work of Christ and the church's participation therein. It may refer specifically to those days in which we celebrate the narrative of passion-death-resurrection; it may be used to speak of the reality and power of Christ in Word and the sacraments; but it also refers to our continuing experience of living with the Lord. It is a rich and powerful concept. In this light we may claim that a genuine recovery of the wholeness of the Paschal Mystery in our worship will bring a deeper personal commitment to the lordship of Christ in our common life, and a deeper sense of what it is to be the church.

At the center of our worship and proclamation is the story of God's whole history with humankind, brought to focus in the passion, death, and resurrection of Christ. Since the beginning of the church's worship, these events have given shape and meaning to the week, the whole year, and even to each day of the Christian's existence. In remembering the mystery of our redemption in Christ through all seasons of the gospel, we proclaim his death until Christ comes in the fullness of glory. Without living memory of who Jesus was and what he accomplished, there would be neither church nor any distinctive Christian identity in the world. It is essential to our common faith and life to enact and to show forth the full and dynamic meaning of dying and rising with Christ. This is precisely what the seasons of Lent and Easter-Pentecost set before us each year.

Purposes of This Book

The main purpose of this book is both simple and far-reaching. Here we present for local church study and use an integrated series of services of worship with pastoral commentary. They move from Ash Wednesday at the beginning of Lent, through the dramatic narrative of Palm/Passion Sunday, Maundy Thursday, and Good Friday, to the crown and summit of the year in the great celebrations of Easter; then on into the continuing exaltation of Jesus as Lord (resurrection, ascension, and the giving of the Holy Spirit) throughout the Great Fifty Days, beginning Easter Day and going through the Day of Pentecost. These worship resources are intended as an invitation and guide for the renewal and deepening of our corporate worship through the time from "ashes to fire." Here is proposed a means of restoring the full Easter-Pentecost season of the Great Fifty Days. This emphasis upon participation in the Lord's saving acts—especially death and resurrection—is not a new idea, though it may be unfamiliar in the worship practices and theology of many of our churches. In fact, these theological themes are the very essence of the gospel as lived and celebrated by the church in its earliest times. The reality and power of the Easter gospel can never be confined to a special set of services; yet it is given a particular intensity during this season. The recovery of this living reality is essential to the renewal of Christian worship and life, and it is the theological foundation of all that has appeared in previous volumes of the Supplemental Worship Resources series.

The patterns, rites, and texts presented in this book are rooted in Christian tradition and are ecumenical in spirit; yet they are also attuned to contemporary needs and the pastoral situation of United Methodist parishes. It is our conviction that the reform and renewal of our worship depends in great measure upon the proclamation of the Paschal Mystery[1] in its fullness. In this we join our sisters and brothers in the great family of Christian communities who also are seeking a more faithful and authentic participation in the redemptive action of Christ our Passover.

The liturgical and theological restoration of this season has been a prime factor in the recovery of what is basic to the worship of Christian people everywhere. For example, the current reformation of Roman Catholic worship following Vatican II received great impetus from the reforms of Holy Week in the 1950s. During the past two decades, Episcopalians, Lutherans, and various Reformed traditions have also given much attention to rethinking Holy Week and Easter, with its Lenten period of preparation. Of great interest to many United Methodists is the new provision of resources for the seasons of Lent and Easter in the new Episcopal *Book of Common Prayer (Proposed)*. In every case, Christian denominations are looking back to some of the earlier patterns of worship in the apostolic and postapostolic church for guidance and insight.

United Methodists have always regarded Holy Week with seriousness and Easter with joy. Much of Wesleyan hymnody attests to this. However, the theological and biblical poverty of our Easter celebrations has often not

been worthy of Wesley's "Christ the Lord is risen today."
Our observance of Holy Week, especially of Maundy
Thursday and Good Friday, are characteristically solemn—the penitential focus of the whole year. We have
been somewhat uncertain about what to do liturgically and
spiritually with the lenten period. Seriously, United
Methodists do not have a rich understanding and practice
of Lent as a time of preparing candidates for Christian
initiation, and a churchwide preparation for Easter.
Furthermore, we are just beginning to understand the
reality of extending the Easter season through the Great
Fifty Days, culminating in the Day of Pentecost. This is
partly a matter of insufficient knowledge of Christian
worship, and partly a lack of appreciation for a full biblical
theology (passion–death–resurrection–ascension–pentecost) with its implications for our worship and common life
in the world.

Underlying the purpose of this book is a fundamental
conviction concerning the nonverbal, dramatic witness of
Christian worship during the Lent-Easter seasons. We have
learned in recent years the value of drama within worship.
More importantly, however, we have come to understand
the inherently dramatic nature of *Christian worship* itself: it
is the action of Christ in the midst of his gathered people,
who respond in harmony with the Holy Spirit, in the Word
and the sign-actions of the sacraments. More and more
pastors and congregations sense the need for this deeper
nonverbal dimension of enactment and participation in the
ongoing action of Christ, beyond hearing words *about* the
gospel.

There is a special dramatic quality in each of these
services, most notably in Palm/Passion Sunday and the
Easter Triduum (sunset of Maundy Thursday to sunset
Easter Day). It is no accident that medieval drama
originated in the readings of the resurrection narratives in

Christian worship. Recovering the range and sweep of the death and resurrection in Jesus Christ reveals the dramatic character of all human life lived in and through him. Thus, the use of these resources should be accompanied by special attention to how forms of nonverbal communication may be employed as means to a living encounter with Christ, and to worship "in spirit and in truth."

Such forms of communication and encounter may be developed in our use of Scripture as well as in various sign-actions (ashes, palms, footwashing, light and darkness, prayer vigils, and the Baptisms, renewals, and Holy Meals at the Lord's table). While some churches may have resources for more elaborate developments than do others, the aim in all these resources is toward a profound simplicity in the essentials.

As further background to the use of the services which follow, let us consider briefly some implications for the lenten period of preparation; and then some key historical, theological, and practical features of the Easter Triduum (pronounced TRĬ-joo-um); and finally the meaning of the Great Fifty Days.

Some Implications for Lent

Since the seasons of Lent and Easter celebrate the most powerful parts of the story of redemption, we concentrate our attention there. Historically, Lent developed as a seeson of preparing and training persons for initiation into the church at Easter. It has come to be the forty days of preparation of the whole church for the great Paschal celebrations, growing out of the intense period of discipline and instruction of the converts, known as the "catechumenate." This was also the period when those who had been alienated and lapsed from the church could be reconciled and restored to fellowship through prayer and penance. Part of our purpose is to enable congregational recovery of Lent as a time of disciplined preparation of the entire local church in the experiences, life, and doctrine that flow from the realities made present during the Christian Passover at Easter.

The early church attracted so many people because of the transforming love, sustaining strength, and encouragement of its way of life. Their faith made them both free and disciplined in the way of Christ. The reality of prayer, the power of their worship and prophetic mission—founded upon the cross and empty tomb—was the church's great evangel to a confused and brutal world. So today our recovery of the rhythm and pattern of their common discipline and celebration of the Lent-Easter Season is part of being faithful to our evangelical calling. Those vital qualities of faith and life are essential features with the United Methodist heritage as well.

Lent is a time for evangelism and true conversion—a time for growing into Christ through repentance, fellowship, prayer, fasting, and concentration upon our baptismal vocation to be signs of God's kingdom in this world. The themes of repentance and preparation for sharing the death and resurrection of Christ are basic to those preparing for Baptism and Confirmation, and to the whole body of Christians who will renew their baptismal faith during the Easter Season. Lent is not merely "giving up something," but taking upon ourselves the intention and the signs of true participation in the mystery of God-with-us.

Christian initiation begins a lifelong process of being transformed into the life and holiness of our Lord. All this, as the New Testament and the early church plainly taught, is not merely an individual's private experience. It is, rather, a communal reality which is the heartbeat of the church's worship and mission in human history. Thus the whole pattern of practical Christian evangelism is inherent in the meaning of this season: encounter with Christ, instruction, initiation, and growth into Christ. Lent thereby gives a meaning and depth to conversion and to "follow through," so that the seeds of God's Word may fall upon fertile soil.

The recovery of the seasons of Lent and Easter is also a theological journey. Here theology is not divorced from life and practice, but it is the reflective fruition of a deepened communion with God in Christ. Within United Methodism we have an opportunity to regain theological substance that arises in the context of prayer and worship; a theology that focuses upon the fundamentals contained in Christian Baptism, the Lord's Supper, and the living proclamation of the Word. Increasing numbers of lay persons and clergy are seriously asking what can be done to renew and to deepen our theological foundations. The Lent-Easter Season is the obvious starting point for such a journey. Contained within it is the possibility of restoring spiritual discipline and life-giving worship experiences that can be sustained through time. One particularly well-designed program for the whole parish, which we commend for study and use, has been published by the Liturgical Conference in Washington, D.C.[2]

Essential to the best use of these services and resources is the intention of each local church to prepare new converts and members for initiation at Easter. But in so doing, the whole church is to be engaged in a common process of renewal and reliving of conversion. This is a process of praying, of searching the Scriptures, of sharing questions and problems of faith and life, of renewing the meaning of witness and discipleship, of taking penance seriously, and of participating in the key celebrations of worship, culminating in Holy Week and Easter.

Ash Wednesday developed in early medieval times as a day of penitence to mark the beginning of Lent—the forty days of preparation for the Paschal celebrations of Easter. Ash Wednesday is a particular time for new beginnings in the faith, a time for "returning to the Lord." On this day we recall our mortality and wait upon the Lord for a renewing Spirit. This is a time for putting aside the sins and failures of the past in light of who we are yet to become by the grace of God. These resources and services are part of a larger environment of repentance and growth in grace. We are to be tested by the Spirit so that our participation in the meaning of the Easter faith may be authentic, and a true dying and rising with Christ to new life in God.

All this implies that careful planning for these services of worship is crucial. The local pastor cannot and should not do everything required. A significant portion of the congregation must be trained to assume various reponsibilities throughout the whole of the time period covered here, but particularly in preparation for the Easter Triduum, as will be made clear in the commentaries. Much of the planning and preparation can be done as part of the congregation's lenten journey. This may provide a unique opportunity for persons to deepen their individual and corporate appreciation for, and involvement in, the Paschal Mystery. Liturgy becomes the "work of the people of God," as its root meaning suggests; and preparation for worship becomes the occasion for a more richly Christ-centered spirituality to develop.

Yet for all the intensity of Lent, we must seek a whole new pace for the season. Our church activities should not exhaust the congregation with mere "busyness." The point is not to sprint through a series of events, classes, services, and busy work only to collapse the day after Easter. Rather, the discipline of Lent should sustain and refresh us so that we may give full expression to church commitments on through the great Easter-Pentecost Season. The time from Ash Wednesday to Pentecost is also a natural time of the secular year in which many persons give themselves with renewed vigor to church programs. The Easter faith should overflow into our mission to do God's will in the world.

Easter Triduum: The Paschal Event

The aim of these three great days of observance is to dramatize and to proclaim the events of our Lord's passion and death, and to awaken in us a sense of God's ever-present saving power through the cross and resurrection. It is not an occasion for mere sentimental remembrance of past events. It is a *way of participating* in these saving events through a unified sequence of actions, Scripture, and common prayer. By faithful participation in the liturgy of Holy Week and Easter, we encounter Christ who, through his redemptive suffering and death and his triumphal rising, comes to deliver all humanity from bondage and death.

The narrative of Holy Week focuses upon the Paschal Mystery. While the dynamic of Christian life in all seasons is that same mystery, it is manifest with explicit power in the celebrations of Palm/Passion Sunday and especially in the climactic last three days of the week (sunset of Maundy Thursday to sunset Easter Day) known as the Triduum.[3] The early church, following a rigorous fast, celebrated the whole mystery on Easter Eve and into Easter Day in one unified liturgy. Everything was contained into the great Easter Vigil: the reading of the mighty acts of God, the telling of our Lord's passion, the lighting of the new fire and the Paschal (or Easter) candle, the presentation of candidates for Baptism, the full initiation rites with the renewal of baptismal vows for the whole church, and the glorious Easter Communion or Eucharist. Even though we have inherited a pattern of narrating and enacting the sweep of events over several days, our intent should be to dwell within the fundamental unity of Christ's one saving action in the self-giving of his life and his being raised from the dead.

The historical sequences of events was first systematically dramatized over the course of Holy Week in fourth century Jerusalem.[4] We are familiar with that sequence: the triumphal entry into the city; the final days of teaching and confrontation with authorities; the Last Supper in the context of the Passover; the subsequent arrest, trial, and crucifixion on Good Friday; the burial and rest in the tomb; and finally, the resurrection early on the first day of the week. Our worship through Holy Week follows this pattern. We begin with Palm/Passion Sunday. The name derives from a combination of two ideas that are in powerful tension with one another: a triumphal entry of the palm-bearing procession into Jerusalem shouting "Hosanna," and the sober realization that Jesus faces the gathering storm of human sin and death. It is a day of contrast and irony. Here we enter into a reenactment of something Scripture tells us vividly the followers of Jesus and others in Jerusalem did on this day. With the extended reading (or other expression) of the passion account from the Evangelists, we encounter anew the tension and reality of his "royal" procession. In no other week and on no other day of the year do we attend to the recounting of so much detailed history. Our worship on Palm/Passion Sunday is a reliving of the final chapters of Jesus' earthly ministry.

On the minor days from Monday through Thursday afternoon, we continue to read the accounts and to ponder them and to pray. On Thursday evening we relive with the disciples that fellowship meal on the very threshold of the Passover in which Jesus uttered the unforgettable words with the sharing of the bread and the cup—"This is my body," "This is the blood of the new covenant"—and commanded that we forever "Do this in remembrance of me." We experience anew that which was enacted on this extraordinary evening, including (if we choose) the act of mutual servanthood in the washing of feet. This may be followed by a service of Tenebrae in which we recall and symbolize the growing darkness of the next hours' events: betrayal in the garden, arrest, and the condemnation of the trial.

Then, on Friday, we recall the crucifixion and death of Christ by again attending to the narration of events. Here the reality of his death is encountered, a death we remembered also at the beginning of Lent on the day of ashes. But now we experience the anguish of our own sin and evil intensified, and our own complicity in his betrayal. The altar-table is stripped and made bare. We may also enter into the shadows of death by using the form of Tenebrae if it was not used Thursday evening. We keep watch and pray as we move through the time of burial and rest in the tomb. Fasting appropriately marks our watch. We await the unfolding of the great mystery which has been accomplished once-for-all, yet remains an ever-renewing and amazing present reality throughout every age.

Thus, Holy Week—especially in its final days—proclaims and enacts the richness of meaning contained in the whole Paschal Mystery. "Christ our Passover is sacrificed for us: Therefore let us keep the feast" (I Corinthians 5:7). In approaching these services of worship, we should not think of each event as an independent entity, but rather as a continually unfolding unified drama of our salvation.

It is our prayer and hope that these resources will be a means of renewing our faith experience, and that the church's worship may more fully and adequately proclaim "Jesus is Lord." We are not concerned merely with becoming more "formal" or "ceremonial" in our style of worship. The essential reality lying behind the recovery of the Paschal Mystery for our tradition is *theological*. In Christ we pass over from death to life, from the present age to the age which is yet to come in fullness. This is God's grace and doing alone. Just as the Hebrews passed from slavery in Egypt to life in God's promised land, and as Jesus Christ was raised from death to life, so the church proclaims and enacts its faith that, by God's saving grace, we pass from sin and death to life with God. The whole world is in the process of being redeemed. Every time we truly proclaim Christ and celebrate the Meal at his table, we "proclaim the Lord's death until he come." The Paschal Mystery comprehends the entire range of life with God, including the eschatological hope of a new heaven and a new earth.

Black American Christians' experience has kept alive for the whole church the vivid power of the exodus themes of deliverance from death and liberation from slavery. Passover-Easter may be immeasurably deepened by celebrating that experience and using resources of proclamation and song from those traditions. There are also themes in native American and other ethnic traditions that may be drawn from to show the universality of the exodus experience. With respect to Good Friday, we inherit devotions based on the "seven last words" tradition from Peruvian sources; and from the Hispanic cultures of New Mexico and Colorado, the powerful Good Friday art of the *penitentes*.

Easter Day, and the Great Fifty Days of Easter

Holy Week and the Easter celebrations contain the entire gospel of salvation. The First Service of Easter, whether celebrated Easter Eve as the vigil or on Easter in the early morning, is both the source and summit of the entire Christian year. Here we are overwhelmed by God's victory and by the vastness of the divine mercy and love. We proclaim Christ crucified, dead, and buried, risen and exalted as the head of the church—the savior of humanity, and the Lord of all things. The whole faith of the church now comes into focus in the continuing life of union with Christ. That faith lives in expectant hope of the Kingdom in its fullness. Whatever life we have is a reflection of the life of God manifest in Jesus Christ through the power of the Holy Spirit. Hence, cross-resurrection theology can never be separated from the exaltation of Christ and the sending forth of his truth and life in the Holy Spirit of God.

The burst of praise and resurrection joy of Easter permeates the entire period from Easter morning through the Day of Pentecost. This is known as the Great Fifty Days.[5] While Easter is the Sunday of all Sundays, gathering up and transfiguring the narrative of Holy Week, and indeed the whole history of God's mighty works; the resurrection courses through the days and weeks of the Easter Season as a never-ending day—a prolonged and sustained Lord's Day. The Paschal candle, symbolizing the morning star that never sets, should be visible and lighted for every gathering for worship during these days of the Easter-Pentecost Season.

Our celebration of the Paschal feast does not end with Easter Sunday, however. Easter Day intiates the time which transforms the passion of Holy Week: the world of the first creation, subject to sin and death, is becoming the new creation. Easter is the Eighth Day which ushers in the end time, promising the never-ending light of eternal life. Special events may take place this week, particularly in connection with those who have been initiated through Baptism, whether as infants or adults, and with those confirmed. Family worship and devotions may emphasize the Easter appearances of Jesus with the apostles and others, as recorded in the Scriptures. We rejoice as the disciples witness to the experience of the glorified Lord. The whole week and the whole of the fifty days should echo the song of victory. "For we know that Christ being raised from the dead will never die again; death no longer has dominion over him. . . . So you also must consider yourselves dead to sin and alive to God in Christ Jesus" (Romans 6:9, 11 RSV). The Easter "Alleluias" should resound throughout this whole season which unfolds the reality of life in the Spirit. It comes to full consciousness when the whole church celebrates the feast of the new age of the Holy Spirit on the Day of Pentecost. On that day we make explicit again the fact that the gospel is proclaimed in every tongue, in every place, unto all the world.

The contrasts between Lent and Easter-Pentecost are dramatic. Lent is sober, reflective, and watchful. This quality is reflected in the ancient practice of omitting "Alleluias" and "Glorias." On the other hand, Easter is exuberant. This should be expressed visually and musically as well. Leaders of worship should be aware of such contrasts and enable the congregation to participate fully in them.

In planning worship for the Easter-Pentecost Season we must bear in mind the intimate connection between resurrection, the exaltation of the Lord, and the sending of the Holy Spirit which characterizes the Great Fifty Days in the witness of Scripture and in praise. The biblical, historical, and theological bases of this Passover-Pentecost festival time are clear and compelling. While it is not possible to establish with absolute certainty its full observance during the apostolic days of the church, there is little doubt that some of the churches knew such a celebration in the late first or early second century. First Corinthians has been described as a Paschal Letter which testifies to the immediate anticipation of Pentecost (I Corinthians 16:8; see also Acts 20:6, 16). Its resounding phrases may testify to the apostolic observance of the

Easter Pascha: "Christ our Passover is sacrificed. Let us, therefore, celebrate the festival, not with the old leaven of malice and evil, but with the unleavened bread of sincerity and truth" (I Corinthians 5:7-8 RSV). Furthermore, from at least the fourth century on, the church has regarded the reading of Acts as the continuing preaching of the apostles, and the outpouring of the Easter gospel. Saint John Chrysostom called this the "demonstration of the resurrection."

The Passover-Pentecost time is, in essence, one great extended Lords' Day feast. It lifts up all the facets of the redeeming work of God in Christ. The Day of Pentecost is a reliving of all that the Easter Season has come to mean for the people of God. In the Old Testament, Israel celebrated the Feast of Weeks, a day of great thanksgiving for the wheat harvest. In later times this also came to be the day commemorating the giving of the Law on Mount Sinai. These meanings carry over, but are transformed by the church's experience of the outpouring of the Holy Spirit and the giving of the Spirit by Jesus Christ to the disciples in their postresurrrection encounter (John 20). It is a day marking the universality of the new age in which "there is neither Jew nor Greek . . . slave nor free, . . . male nor female; for you all are one in Christ Jesus" (Galatians 3:28 RSV). This shows the new unity in the spirit of the Lord through whom all nations may be reconciled; yet it also celebrates the "birthday" of the church.

Ten days earlier we celebrate Ascension Day—the fortieth day after Easter, based upon the scriptural account of Jesus' forty days on earth following the resurrection, according to Acts 1. We should not, however, think of this as a completely separate historical commemoration. In fact, until at least the end of the fourth century, the ascension of Christ and the descent of the Spirit were celebrated on the same Lord's Day. For us as well, the exaltation of the risen Christ is intimately linked with his giving of the Holy Spirit. As John's Gospel brings out, Jesus must go to the Father in order that the Counselor, the Spirit of Truth, may abide with those who believe and love.

If we use the expression "Season of Pentecost" at all, it is most fittingly applied to the Easter Season itself. The Day of Pentecost is its culmination. Our worship during these days makes manifest what we confess in the Apostles' Creed: "He ascended into heaven and sits at the right hand of God the Father Almighty." Jesus promises not to leave his followers comfortless; this promise is fulfilled. The Holy Spirit comes to teach the church all truth, and to enliven our common remembrance of all that Jesus was and is for us and for the whole world. The Holy Spirit illuminates what is yet to come. "Amen, Come, Lord Jesus!" (Revelation 22:20 RSV)—this is the church's final cry.

For all these reasons, Baptisms and renewals of Baptism are most appropriate on the Day of Pentecost. Tertullian, whose writings reflect second-century practices, mentions that the church normally baptizes on Easter and the Day of Pentecost. However, he goes on to say that any Lord's Day is suitable. In larger congregations, the whole season of the Great Fifty Days is particularly opportune if there are large numbers of families with children or of adult initiates who have undergone instruction and Lenten preparation. Pentecost is the second climax of the Paschal Season; its proper and joyful celebration gives sustaining power to all the "ordinary" time of the season after Pentecost.

From ashes to fire, from repentance to rebirth, from sin and death to resurrection and eternal life: these are the themes we have been given to recover and celebrate again in our common worship. These are the heart of our existence before God. The services and resources which follow invite every local church to worship anew the living Lord, to enact the drama of salvation "in spirit and in truth," and to receive the abundance of God's grace.

II.

Practical Suggestions

There are a number of practical and pastoral considerations that arise in the course of planning worship for Lent and Easter. Most of these are addressed in the commentaries which follow each particular order of service. There are, however, certain elements and forms in these services that may not be familiar to all United Methodists and so deserve special mention at the outset. It is especially important that the presiding minister(s), the choir and musicians, and other lay leaders be "at home" with, and gain a clear understanding of, the elements and forms of worship, so that a full and vital participation of the whole congregation is made possible.

You will discover an extensive use of psalms in these services. The texts of many are printed out; but other translations may be substituted if deemed appropriate. Bear in mind the singability and poetic quality of these texts. In many cases, the psalms will be spoken rather than sung; but there are several effective ways of doing the psalms. They may be subdivided into larger sections and read alternately by various sections of the congregation. Or, they may be said or sung responsively between a leader or the choir and the people.

Many congregations are becoming familiar with various settings of the psalms such as those of Lucien Deiss, the Gelineau version, and the more recent Lutheran settings.[6] One very simple mode is to chant the psalm responsively on a single tone with a rising or falling tone at the end of each line. In other cases, a new setting may be composed by the organist or other musician in the local church, suitable to the particular choir and congregation's musical abilities. Familiarity with versified psalms in the hymnal may suggest further variations (see the listing of psalms in the Index of Scripture References of Hymns in the *Book of Hymns* 847).

In most cases there are *antiphons* with each psalm. These are verses from within the psalm that express a main theme. The antiphon is first recited or sung by the leader or choir, and the congregation immediately responds with the same line. Then the psalm is prayed, at the conclusion of which the antiphon is recited or sung by all. In longer psalms the antiphon may be used after each verse or particular grouping of verses. This responsorial style helps the congregation to focus and participate in the whole psalm without having to recite or sing it all. This also allows for greater musical flexibility on the part of the leader or the choir. A brief rehearsal of the antiphons before the service begins will put the congregation at ease. Congregations are increasingly finding new joy and depth in the recovery of sung psalmody in worship. We recommend the book, *Psalms in Christian Worship,* by Massey Shepherd, Jr., (Minneapolis: Augsburg Press; and Collegeville, Minn.: Liturgical Press, 1976) as an excellent introduction for local church use.

The *responsories* are also new features in some of these

services. These are intended to focus the congregational response to Scripture. Each is specifically related to the lections for the day, and is composed of scriptural phrases which speak a theme or set of images. The congregation and a leader may recite them in responsive style. Again, musicians are encouraged to compose simple musical settings for them.

Throughout all these worship services the choir plays a significant leadership role, especially by reciting or singing the psalms and responses with the congregation. The song leader or cantor will be of considerable assistance to the congregation where the ministers do not have ability to inspire confidence in leading singing. The choir director may, of course, be the leader of congregational song as well.

Generally speaking, the range and depth of these services depend in great measure upon the recovery of congregational song and the ease of participation in various psalms and responses. A gracious way of introducing these elements and of rehearsing them with the choir and the people is essential. In some cases this may be done before the service begins; in others it may be introduced at other gatherings, such as at family night suppers or group meetings. In any event, the worship committee should be among the first to learn them, and to appreciate the variety of ways these may be integrated into a congregation's worship experience.

A study of these services also reveals the wide range of congregational movement and gesture which may be encouraged. Movements such as processions, coming to receive ashes or the bread and cup, are powerful means of participation in and communicating the gospel. These services invite physical movement on the days of high drama such as Palm/Passion Sunday and in the Good

Friday and Easter services. These may be done with grace and genuine spontaneous power *if* they are introduced confidently and simply. The movements should be natural and unaffected; not regimented, yet clearly intentional. This may require a brief rehearsal with some members of the congregation, and especially the choir, beforehand.

Since congregational processions are not an every-Sunday event; careful planning must be given to the logistics of space and time. Processions may include banners, the cross, the Bible, and other items, such as candles and vessels which may be used in the service. It is particularly helpful to allow the musicians to lead such processions, and to use strong instruments, such as the trumpet, when outside the building.

Special provision should be made to include the elderly, or persons unable to walk, by encouraging the use of wheelchairs. This may even contribute to renovating entranceways so that persons with crutches or in wheelchairs can enter easily. This can be a powerful witness to the gospel. Very small children and infants can be carried. Children, of course, understand processions and bodily movements better than grownups, and are often eager to learn and to share in the meaning of festive processions.

Lent and Easter provide rich possibilities in the use of visuals, textures, graphics, and banners. Those planning these services should give careful attention to the helpful suggestions found in *Seasons of the Gospel* (Supplemental Worship Resources 6). If specific questions arise concerning other aspects of these services, you may wish to write directly for further assistance to the Section on Worship, PO Box 840, Nashville, Tennessee 37202. Lists of Lenten and Easter-Pentecost music, both choral and instrumental, may also be obtained by writing to the Section on Worship.

In preparing the bulletin or the people's texts, the

complete outline and all the prayers of the service need *not* be included. Only the essentials need be printed: the basic common prayer texts, responses, psalms with antiphons (or just the antiphons when the psalms are done responsorially), and other hymns and music that cannot be found in *The Book of Hymns.* The pages need not be cluttered with unnecessary rubrics or optional texts. The full text of the Great Thanksgiving at Holy Communion, for example, is not absolutely needed; only the unison parts for the congregation with the lead-in lines. If the whole order must be printed, keep it simple.

The cover should express the theme, and may use a symbol or set of drawings that are part of the theological meaning of the service. Encourage creativity, yet restraint. Occasionally members of the congregation may contribute special drawings, photographs, or other graphics for reproduction. We should aim at integration of the visual experience of the bulletin and the environment of the room and the liturgy. If slides are employed in the intercessions, for example, a representative one may be used for the cover.

Special thought should be given to introducing and concluding the readings from Scripture. Lections may be immediately preceded by such words as "Hear the Word of God in a reading from _____." In closing, the reader may say: "This is the Word of the Lord," or "The Word of the Lord," or simply "Amen." Some congregations wish to respond by saying, "Thanks be to God." Some may introduce the Gospel readings by saying, "A reading from the Gospel according to _____," with the congregation responding, "Glory be to you, Lord." The concluding phrase may be, "The Gospel of the Lord," with the people responding, "Praise to you, Lord Jesus Christ."

Finally, persons preparing these services should study and discuss *Word and Table* (Abingdon, 1976), and *A*

Service of Baptism, Confirmation, and Renewal (The United Methodist Publishing House, 1976), since the sacramental actions of the Lord's Supper and Baptism are at the heart of the Paschal Mystery we are to celebrate and live during these seasons.

III.

Ash Wednesday:
An Order of Worship
with Commentary

GATHERING   *In silence and meditation.*
*If a brief exposition of the service is necessary, it may be
done quietly during this time, allowing for a return to
silence before the greeting. If a choir is to process, let it be
done in silence just prior to the greeting.*

GREETING
The grace of our Lord Jesus Christ be with you.

And also with you.

Bless the Lord, O my soul,
and all that is within me, bless God's holy name.

**Bless the Lord, O my soul,
and forget not all God's benefits.**

Who forgives all your sins
and heals all your infirmities;

**Who redeems your life from the grave,
and crowns you with mercy and loving-kindness.**

OPENING PRAYER

Let us pray: *A brief silence.*

Most Holy God,
   your Son came to save sinners;
We come to this season of repentance,
   confessing our unworthiness,
   asking for new and honest hearts,
   and the healing power of your forgiveness.
Grant this through Christ our Lord. **Amen.**

or

Almighty and everlasting God,
   you hate nothing you have made
   and forgive the sins of all who are penitent:
Create and make in us new and contrite hearts,
   that we, worthily lamenting our sins
   and acknowledging our wretchedness,
   may obtain of you, the God of all mercy,
   perfect remission and forgiveness;
Through Jesus Christ our Lord,
   who lives and reigns with you and the Holy Spirit,
   one God, for ever and ever. **Amen.**

HYMN ["Lord, Who Throughout These Forty Days,"
tune: ST. FLAVIAN or other CM]

1. Lord, who throughout these forty days,
      For us didst fast and pray,
   Teach us with thee to mourn our sins,
      And close by thee to stay.

2. As thou with Satan did contend,
      and didst the vict'ry win,
   O give us strength in thee to fight,
      In thee to conquer sin.

3. And through these days of penitence,
      And through thy Passiontide,

35

Yea, evermore, in life and death,
　　Jesus! with us abide.

4. Abide with us, that so, this life
　　Of suffering overpast,
　An Easter of unending joy
　　We may attain at last! Amen.

FIRST LECTION
　Joel 2:12-19　　　　　　　(Year A: 1981, 1984, 1987)
　Isaiah 58:1-12　　　　　　(Year B: 1979, 1982, 1985)
　Zechariah 7:4-10　　　　　(Year C: 1980, 1983, 1986)

PSALM 103:8-18 *Or entire, sung or recited.*
　Antiphon: **The Lord is full of compassion and mercy.**
　The Lord is full of compassion and merc;,
　　slow to anger and of great kindness.

　He will not always accuse us,
　　nor will he keep his anger for ever.

　He has not dealt with us according to our sins,
　　nor rewarded us according to our wickedness.

　For as the heavens are high above the earth,
　　so is his mercy great upon those who fear him.

　As far as the east is from the west,
　　so far has he removed our sins from us.

　As a father cares for his children,
　　so does the Lord care for those who fear him.

　For he knows whereof we are made;
　　he remembers that we are but dust.

　Our days are like the grass;
　　we flourish like a flower of the field;

　When the wind goes over it, it is gone,
　　and its place shall know it no more.

36

But the merciful goodness of the Lord endures for ever
on those who fear him,
and his righteousness on children's children;

On those who keep his covenant
and remember his commandments and do them.

Antiphon: **The Lord is full of compassion and mercy.**

SECOND LECTION

II Corinthians 5:20b–6:10	(Year A: 1981, 1984, 1987)
James 1:12-18	(Year B: 1979, 1982, 1985)
I Corinthians 9:19-27	(Year C: 1980, 1983, 1986)

RESPONSE
Cry, and God will answer.

Call, and the Lord will say: "I am here."

If you do away with the yoke,
the clenched fist, the wicked word;
If you give your bread to the hungry,
and relief to the oppressed;

Call, and the Lord will say; "I am here."

Your light will rise in the darkness,
and your shadows become like noon.
The Lord will always guide you,
giving you relief in desert places.

Cry, and God will answer
Call, and the Lord will say; "I am here."

THE GOSPEL

Matthew 6:1-6, 16-21	(Year A: 1981, 1984, 1987)
Mark 2:15-20	(Year B: 1979, 1982, 1985)
Luke 5:29-35	(Year C: 1980, 1983, 1986)

SERMON

37

INVITATION TO THE OBSERVANCE
OF LENTEN DISCIPLINE

The following or similar words may be spoken.

Dear brothers and sisters in Christ: Christians have always observed with great devotion the days of our Lord's passion and resurrection. It became the custom of the church to prepare for Easter by a season of penitence, fasting, and prayer. This season of forty days provided a time in which converts to the faith were prepared for Baptism into the body of Christ. It is also the time when persons who had committed serious sins and had been separated from the community of faith were reconciled by penitence and forgiveness, and restored to the fellowship of the church. The whole congregation is thus reminded of the mercy and forgiveness proclaimed in the gospel of Jesus Christ and the need we all have to renew our baptismal faith.

I invite you, in the name of the Lord, to observe a holy Lent, by self-examination, penitence, prayer, fasting, and almsgiving; and by reading and meditating on the Word of God. To make a right beginning, and as a mark of our mortality, let us now kneel (bow) before our Creator and Redeemer.

A brief silence is kept.

THANKSGIVING OVER THE ASHES

The Lord be with you.

And also with you.

Let us pray:
Almighty God,
   you have created us out of the dust of the earth;
Grant that these ashes may be to us a sign of our
   mortality and penitence, so we may remember that

only by your gracious gift are we given everlasting
life;

Through Jesus Christ our Savior. **Amen.**

IMPOSITION OF ASHES
*Suitable hymns or psalms may be sung during the
imposition, or it may be done in silence.*

Remember that you are dust, and to dust you shall
return.

and/or

Repent, and believe the gospel.

A PSALM OF CONFESSION   Psalm 51:1-17
Have mercy on me, O God, according to your
      loving-kindness;
   in your great compassion blot out my offenses.
Wash me through and through from my wickedness
   and cleanse me from my sin.

For I know my transgressions,
   and my sin is ever before me.
Against you only have I sinned
   and done what is evil in your sight.

And so you are justified when you speak
   and upright in your judgment.
Indeed, I have been wicked from my birth,
   a sinner from my mother's womb.
For behold, you look for truth deep within me,
   and will make me understand wisdom secretly.

Purge me from my sin, and I shall be pure;
   wash me, and I shall be whiter than snow.
Make me hear of joy and gladness,
   that the body you have broken may rejoice.

Hide your face from my sins
   and blot out all my iniquities.

Create in me a clean heart, O God,
and renew a right spirit within me.

Cast me not away from your presence
and take not your holy Spirit from me.
Give me the joy of your saving help again
and sustain me with your bountiful Spirit.
I shall teach your ways to the wicked,
and sinners shall return to you.

Deliver me from death, O God,
and my tongue shall sing of your righteousness,
O God of my salvation.

Open my lips, O Lord,
and my mouth shall proclaim your praise.
Had you desired it, I would have offered sacrifice,
but you take no delight in burnt-offering.
The sacrifice of God is a troubled spirit;
a broken and contrite heart, O God,
you will not despise.

ABSOLUTION, or RECONCILIATION AND COMMENDATION

The minister may say:

The Almighty and merciful God, Source of our salvation in Christ, who desires not the death of a sinner but rather that we turn from wickedness and live; accept your repentance, forgive your sins, and restore you by the Holy Spirit to newness of life. **Amen.**

Or the following mutual pardon may be exchanged between pastor and people.

In the name of Jesus Christ, you are forgiven!

In the name of Jesus Christ, you are forgiven!

Rejoicing in the fellowship of all the saints,
let us commend ourselves, one another, and our whole
life to Christ our Lord.

To you, O Lord.

PRAYERS OF THE PEOPLE
Responding: **Lord, have mercy,** *or* **Have mercy on your
people.**

THE PEACE
The peace of the Lord be with you all.

And also with you.
All may exchange signs of peace and reconciliation.

OFFERING
*If the Lord's Supper is not celebrated, the service may
conclude with a brief prayer of thanksgiving, followed by:*

THE LORD'S PRAYER

HYMN

DISMISSAL WITH BLESSING
Go forth into the world in the strength of God's mercy to
live and serve in newness of life.

We are sent in Christ's name.

May Jesus Christ, the bread of heaven, bless and keep us.

Amen.

May the Lamb of God who laid down his life for all,
graciously smile upon us.

Amen.

May the Lord our God order all our days and deeds in
peace.

Amen.   Thanks be to God.

41

*
**   **   **
*   *   *

TAKING THE BREAD AND CUP

If the Lord's Supper is celebrated, the table may be prepared while a hymn is sung. The gifts are presented and the service continues with the Great Thanksgiving.

GREAT THANKSGIVING

The Lord be with you.

And also with you.

Lift up your hearts.

We lift them to the Lord.

Let us give thanks to the Lord our God.

It is right to give him thanks and praise.

It is right, and a good and joyful thing always and everywhere to give you thanks, Father Almighty, creator of heaven and earth. You bid your faithful people cleanse their hearts, and prepare with joy for the Paschal feast; that, fervent in prayer and works of mercy, and renewed by your Word and sacraments, we may come to the fullness of grace which you have prepared for those who love you.

Therefore we join the whole of your family in heaven and on earth, for ever praising you and saying (singing):

**Holy, holy, holy Lord, God of power and might,
Heaven and earth are full of your glory.
Hosanna in the highest.
Blessed is he who comes in the name of the Lord.
Hosanna in the highest.**

Most holy and gracious God:
In infinite love you made us for yourself;

and when we had fallen into sin
and become subject to evil and death,
in the fullness of time you sent Jesus Christ,
your only Son, to redeem the world,
to live and to die as one of us, but without sin,
to reconcile us to you and to one another.
He stretched out his arms upon the cross,
and there offered himself, in obedience to your will,
a perfect sacrifice for the sins of the whole world.

On the night he was delivered to suffering and death,
our Lord Jesus took bread;
when he had given thanks to you,
he broke it, and gave it to his disciples, saying:
"Take, eat: This is my body, which is given for you.
Do this for the remembrance of me."
After supper he took the cup;
and giving thanks, he gave it to them, saying:
"Drink this, all of you: This is my blood of the new
    covenant,
shed for you and for all, for the forgiveness of sins.
Whenever you drink it, do this for the remembrance of
    me."

We celebrate the memorial of our redemption, most holy
    God,
in this sacrifice of praise and thanksgiving.
Recalling his death, resurrection, and ascension,
we offer you these gifts which you have given.
Sanctify them by your Holy Spirit
to be for us the body and blood of your Son,
the gracious food and drink of new and unending life.
Sanctify us that we may faithfully receive this sacrament,
and serve you in unity, fidelity, and peace;
and at the last bring us with all your saints

into the joy of your eternal kingdom,
Through Jesus Christ our Lord.

**Through him, with him, in him,
in the unity of the Holy Spirit,
all honor and glory is yours, Almighty God,
now and for ever.   Amen.**

With the confidence of children, let us pray:
Our Father . . .
                    All pray the Lord's Prayer.

THE BREAKING OF THE BREAD

COMMUNION   *Choir and congregation may sing.*
**Lamb of God, you take away the sins of the world;
    Have mercy on us.
Lamb of God, you take away the sins of the world;
    Have mercy on us.
Lamb of God, you take away the sins of the world;
    Grant us peace.**
                        or
**Jesus, Lamb of God,
    have mercy on us.
Jesus, bearer of our sins,
    have mercy on us.
Jesus, redeemer of the world,
    give us your peace.**

PRAYER AFTER COMMUNION
Gracious and holy Lord,
    we give you thanks for healing us
    and feeding us once again.
As Jesus Christ gave his life to us and for all,
    so may we give ourselves to others
    by the power of your Holy Spirit.   **Amen.**

HYMN OR DOXOLOGICAL STANZA

DISMISSAL WITH BLESSING

Go forth into the world in the strength of God's mercy
to live and to serve in newness of life.
May Jesus Christ, the bread of heaven, bless and keep
you.

Amen.

May the Lamb of God who laid down his life for all,
graciously smile upon you.

Amen.

May the Lord God order all your days and deeds in
peace.

Amen. Thanks be to God.
All may depart in quietness.

Commentary

Ash Wednesday emphasizes a dual encounter: we
confront our own mortality and confess our sins before God
within the community of faith. The form of the service and
the texts presented here are designed to focus our lives
upon the dual themes of sin and death in light of God's
redeeming love in Jesus Christ. While the use of ashes as a
sign of mortality and penance may be new to some United
Methodists, they have a significant history in Jewish and
Christian worship. The imposition of ashes is a powerful
nonverbal and experiential way of participating in the call
to repentance and reconciliation. This day can become in
some manner a Yom Kippur, or Day of Atonement for the
Christian community.

In some circumstances, this service may be held early in
the morning, before the school and workday begin.
Noonday is an especially suitable time, since many persons
can attend from home, school, or work, and begin to

observe a fast with the deletion of the regular noon meal. An early evening hour, following a shared sacrificial meal of bread and water, is also appropriate. Pastoral considerations should be given to the local situation in order to determine the best time and place, in the event no custom has already been established. Where more than one service is necessary in a church, modifications of the length of service can easily be made.

The tone and atmosphere is sober and meditative. The sanctuary or room of worship should be appropriately austere and quiet (see *Seasons of the Gospel,* p. 68, for suggestions). On this occasion, silence should be experienced along with the gravity of the Scripture readings. If a cross is used in silent procession with the choir (or just with the ministers), it may be held a moment before each section of the congregation before being placed in a floor holder near the center of the actions which follow. Focus should be upon the reading of Scripture, the prayers, and the simple ritual actions with the ashes.

Various means of participation in the symbolism and sign actions with the ashes may be considered. Here is one well-tested example: After the opening hymn, but before the Scripture lections, ushers may distribute small cards or pieces of paper. These may also be picked up upon entering the room. Each person, having been instructed at the beginning of the service, may then write down before the end of the sermon a particular sin or characteristic in his or her life which is hurtful or unjust to others. These cards will then be brought by each person in procession (or by the ushers) following the sermon and placed upon a grate, to be burned with palm branches for the ashes. If this is done, preparations for the burning (a receptacle for the ashes, and the like) should be made well in advance of the service, and the grate should be set in a visible place before the congregation.

If the ashes are prepared in advance, care should be taken to use palms or other leaves that produce a black or very dark ash. Pulverizing may be necessary. Light-colored ashes reduce the power of the symbolic cross mark.

It is essential that the whole service be permeated by genuine prayer. The sermon need not be long—eight to ten minutes at most—since the readings from Scripture and the penitential actions are themselves proclamatory. Alternative modes of proclamation include: (1) a choral setting of the main themes; (2) silent meditation upon a few well-chosen slides or other visuals portraying mortality and penance (wilderness, desert, images of sin and human injury, injustice, reconciliation, water, wind and dust, oasis); (3) dramatic reading of Luke 3:1-17 (three readers: a narrator, John the Baptist, and the remaining sections—prophecy from Isaiah and the various questions). This may be substituted for the Gospel reading, and may be followed by silence or a brief choral meditation or a suitable hymn; (4) a period of silence for examination of conscience, directed with appropriate sentences or readings.

The central congregational action, apart from the Lord's Supper, if celebrated, is the rite of imposition of ashes. Particular sensitivity and grace must be exercised in the manner in which this is done. After the prayer over the ashes, the minister(s) and assistant(s) take their places at a focal point in the room and indicate with a gesture for the first rows of the congregation to come forward. The minister, and assistant(s), if any, make a cross of ashes on each forehead with the thumb, saying, "Remember that you are dust, and to dust you shall return," and/or "Repent, and believe the gospel." These could be said alternately.

A sense of solemnity and freedom is desired, no matter how humble or elaborate the church building. Ushering people stiffly, row by row, should be avoided. In a small congregation, people may simply come forward to the altar rail, kneel or stand to receive, and return by a side aisle to their seats. A continuously moving, yet unrushed, line is best. Those waiting may remain seated or bowed, and rise in turn; those returning may join in singing, if hymns are used. In large congregations, there may be two or more "stations" at which ministers and assistants are standing. Worshipers in each section will come forward and then return to their seats by the opposite end of the pew or row. If there is a choir, those persons may receive first and then return to lead in the singing of hymns or psalms (most suitably, Psalms 23, 130, and 32).

The confession of sin takes the form of communal recital of Psalm 51. Following the return of the last person from the imposition of ashes, all should stand or kneel. The psalm may be read responsively between the minister and the people or by a leader and choir alternating with the people, or between two sections of the congregation. The particular style or grouping of the verses may be designated in the printed text. In some cases it may be possible to sing or chant the psalm to a simple tune or psalm-tone setting.

The confession of sins is followed by a brief silence, and then a general absolution or a reconciliation and commendation—depending upon which is more appropriate to local convictions. The intercessions that follow should always include petitions for the church universal and for the brokenness of the world, emphasizing both social and personal dimensions of repentance and of solidarity with human suffering. Whenever possible prepared petitions should be included along with time for spontaneous ones. A simple form for congregational response to each petition, such as "Lord, have mercy" or "Have mercy on your people," may be used. The minister or assistant would begin, "Most merciful God, hear our prayers for others as we say, 'Lord, have mercy.' " Then may follow petitions, such as "For the victims of our sin, and all who bear the burden of our faults, let us pray to the Lord;" the congregation responding, "Lord have mercy." And so on.

It is also possible to use a visual litany, each image or slide being responded to in the manner indicated above. For example, the images in Matthew 25 may be used, along with questions, such as "Lord, when did we see you . . . ?" or "Is it nothing to you, all you who pass by?"

The gravity and pace of this service may not lend itself to the inclusion of the Sacrament of the Lord's Supper. It may, however, be celebrated as an integral part of the whole liturgy. The text of the Great Thanksgiving presented above may be replaced by the version found in Service 830 in the *Book of Hymns*. If the Sacrament is not celebrated, the congregation and choir still may wish to sing one of the several settings of the *Agnus Dei* ("Lamb of God") found in the *Book of Hymns* in place of a closing hymn. This may give a powerful unity to the service as it comes to a conclusion. If there is both the imposition of ashes and a celebration of Communion, these should always be separated, with the people coming forward for each particular action.

When a final hymn or other sung response is used, it may be sung before the dismissal with blessing while the ministers remain facing the congregation. The choir and ministers may then recess in silence with the cross going before them. The people depart in silence.

IV.

Palm/Passion Sunday: An Order of Worship with Commentary

Procession with the Palms

The congregation may gather at a designated place outside the church building, or in the fellowship hall or other suitable place. Here palm branches, festive reeds, or green branches are distributed to all, and a brief introduction to the whole service may be given. At the processional hymn, the congregation, musicians, and leaders process into the sanctuary.

MUSIC FOR GATHERING

GREETING   *May be sung by choir and congregation.*
Hosanna to the Son of David, the King of Israel!

**Blessed is he who comes in the name of the Lord.
Hosanna in the highest!**

OPENING PRAYER
The Lord be with you.

And also with you.

Let us pray: *A brief silence is kept.*
God our hope,
today we joyfully acclaim Jesus
    our Messiah and King.
Help us to honor him every day
    so we may enjoy his kingship in the new Jerusalem,
    where he reigns with you and the Holy Spirit
    for ever and ever. **Amen.**

Or, if a thanksgiving over the palms is used.

The Lord be with you.

And also with you.

Let us give thanks to the Lord our God.

It is right to give him thanks and praise.

We praise and bless you, ever-living God,
    for the acts of love by which you redeem the world
    through Jesus Christ our Lord.
This day he entered the holy city of Jerusalem
    and was proclaimed king by those
    who spread their garments and palm branches along
        his way.
Let these branches be for us signs of his victory;
    and grant that we who bear them may always acclaim
        Jesus Messiah
    by walking the way of his suffering and cross;
    that, dying and rising with him, we may enter into
        your kingdom.
Through Jesus Christ, who lives and reigns with you
    and the Holy Spirit, now and forever. **Amen.**

PROCLAMATION OF THE ENTRANCE INTO JERUSALEM

Here is read the Gospel narrative appointed for the year, after which the response is said or sung by all, and the procession begins.

Matthew 21:1-11*a*　　　　(Year A: 1981, 1984, 1987)
Mark 11:1-10　　　　　　(Year B: 1979, 1982, 1985)
Luke 19:28-40　　　　　　(Year C: 1980, 1983, 1986)

Blessed is he who comes in the name of the Lord!

Hosanna in the highest!

PROCESSIONAL HYMN　　　*Hymn 424* or *see* The Book of Hymns, *422-25, 88, 363, and 482.*

The celebration of the Word of God.

PRAYER FOR ILLUMINATION　　*Congregation remains standing.*

God our Redeemer,

　you sent your Son to be born of a woman
　and to die for us on a cross;

By your Holy Spirit, illumine our lives with your Word
　so, as the Scripture is read and proclaimed this day,
　we may be reconciled and won wholly to your will;

Through Jesus Christ our Lord. **Amen.**

FIRST LECTION
　Isaiah 50:4-9*a*　　　　　(Year A: 1981, 1984, 1987)
　Zechariah 9:9-12　　　　(Year B: 1979, 1982, 1985)
　Deuteronomy 32:36-39　　(Year C: 1980, 1983, 1986)

PSALM OR ANTHEM
　Psalm 22:1-11　　　　　　(Year A: 1981, 1984, 1987)
　Psalm 22:7-8, 16-19, 22-23 (Year B: 1979, 1982, 1985)
　Psalm 31:1-5, 9-16　　　　(Year C: 1980, 1983, 1986)

SECOND LECTION   Philippians 2:5-11 (Years A,B,C)

A PASSION HYMN   *See* Book of Hymns, *412-25, especially 76.*

PROCLAMATION OF THE PASSION STORY
  Matthew 26:14–27:66   (Year A: 1981, 1984, 1987)
  Mark 14:1–15:47   (Year B: 1979, 1982, 1985)
  Luke 22:1–23:56   (Year C: 1980, 1983, 1986)

[SERMON]   *See commentary for various modes of proclamation with detailed suggestions.*

Responses and Offerings

CONCERNS AND PRAYERS OF THE PEOPLE

THE PEACE

OFFERING   *When the Lord's Supper is not celebrated, the service concludes with the following.*

PRAYER OF THANKSGIVING and THE LORD'S PRAYER

HYMN

DISMISSAL WITH BLESSING
  May Jesus Christ, the bread of heaven broken for all,
    bless you and keep you.

  Amen.

  May the Lamb of God who takes away the sins of the
      world,
    heal and restore you.

  Amen.

  May the Lord God order all your days and deeds in
      peace.

  Amen.

Go in love to serve God and your neighbor in all things.

Amen. Thanks be to God.

*   *   *
**   **   **

OFFERING   *When the Sacrament of the Lord's Supper is to be celebrated, the gifts of bread and wine may be presented with the offering, the table having been prepared during the singing of a hymn or anthem of a suitable text.*

THE GREAT THANKSGIVING

The Lord be with you.

And also with you.

Lift up your hearts.

We lift them to the Lord.

Let us give thanks to the Lord our God.

It is right to give him thanks and praise.

It is right, and a good and joyful thing,
always and everywhere to give you thanks,
Father Almighty, creator of heaven and earth.
You brought all things into being and called them good.
From the dust of the earth you formed us into your
    image,
and breathed into us the breath of life.
When we turned away, and our love failed,
your love remained steadfast.
You delivered us from slavery and made us your people,
calling us to life through Moses and all the prophets.

Therefore we join the whole of your family,
in heaven and on earth,
for ever praising you and saying (singing):

54

Holy, holy, holy Lord, God of power and might.
Heaven and earth are full of your glory.
Hosanna in the highest.
Blessed is he who comes in the name of the Lord.
Hosanna in the highest.

Blessed are you, O Lord our God,
for when your Son was sent to save us,
he laid aside his glory and became one of us,
entering into human temptations and trials,
eating with sinners, yet without sin,
he took upon himself our sin and death.
For us he was lifted high upon the cross,
that he might draw the whole world to himself;
and, by his suffering and death,
became the source of eternal salvation
for all who put their trust in God.

On the night his disciples betrayed and deserted him,
he took bread, gave you thanks, broke it,
gave it to them, and said:
"Take, eat, this is my body which is given for you."
After the supper, he took the cup, gave you thanks,
gave it to his disciples, and said:
"Drink from this, all of you,
this is my blood, which seals God's promise,
poured out for you and for all, for the forgiveness of
    sins."

When we eat this bread and drink from this cup
we receive anew the presence of Christ
and look forward to his coming in final victory.
Receiving anew all you have accomplished for us in Jesus
    Christ,
we offer our sacrifice of praise and thanksgiving,
presenting these gifts which you have given.

We remember his death,
We proclaim his resurrection,
We await his coming in glory!

Send your Holy Spirit upon us
and upon these gifts of bread and wine,
that the sharing of this bread may be
a participation in the body of the living Christ,
and the sharing of this cup a participation in his blood,
that we may serve you in unity, fidelity, and joy
until you bring us with all your saints into
the fullness of your eternal kingdom;
Through Jesus Christ our Lord.

Through him, with him, in him,
in the unity of the Holy Spirit,
all glory and honor is yours, Almighty God,
for ever and ever. Amen.

With the confidence of children we pray:

THE LORD'S PRAYER   **Our Father . . .**

THE BREAKING OF THE BREAD

THE GIVING OF BREAD AND THE CUP
Choir and congregation may sing the following and/or
suitable hymns during Communion.

Lamb of God, you take away the sins of the world,
Have mercy on us.
Lamb of God, you take away the sins of the world,
Have mercy on us.
Lamb of God, you take away the sins of the world,
Grant us peace.

or

Jesus, Lamb of God,
have mercy on us.

56

Jesus, bearer of our sins,
have mercy on us.
Jesus, redeemer of the world,
give us your peace.

PRAYER AFTER COMMUNION
Lord,
we give you thanks for satisfying our hungry hearts
with this holy meal shared in the Spirit with your Son;
As his death brings us life and hope,
so may his resurrection lead us to salvation;
This we ask through Jesus Christ our Lord. **Amen.**

HYMN or DOXOLOGICAL STANZA

DISMISSAL WITH BLESSING
May Jesus Christ, the bread of heaven broken for all,
bless you and keep you.

Amen.

May the Lamb of God, who takes away the sins of the
world,
heal and restore you.

Amen.

May the Lord God order all your days and deeds in
peace.

Amen.

Go in love to serve God and your neighbor in all things.

Amen. Thanks be to God.

Commentary
The church's worship on this day is inherently dramatic.
It provides us with many possibilities for proclaiming the

Word of God and entering fully into the events recalled this day. The proclamatory readings and the presentation of the narrative of our Lord's Passion is the heart of the service of the Word. We experience more Scripture in public worship today than on almost any other occasion of the year.

This is why Palm/Passion Sunday is not a particularly suitable day for celebrating Baptism, Confirmation, or the reception of new members. It is strongly advised that Baptisms and Confirmations (first renewal of baptismal vows) be celebrated during the Easter Vigil or the First Service of Easter, or on any of the Sundays during the season of the Great Fifty Days between Easter and the Day of Pentecost. See the Introduction of this book and the first chapter of *Seasons of the Gospel* for further theological guidance.

The structure of this service is simple, focusing in four principal sections: the procession with the palms, the celebration of the Word of God (passion), responses and offerings, and the Sacrament of the Lord's Supper. Though many United Methodist congregations have not celebrated Communion on this day in the recent past, it is to be encouraged, since this is a natural completion of the whole narrative flow of the Word of God; hence, the completion of our participation in the salvation wrought by Christ's passion, death, and resurrection. Congregations should be made aware that on this particular occasion, the service may be longer than on a usual Lord's Day.

It is a day of contrasts. In the first part we experience the joyous demonstration of loyalty to Jesus, who "comes in the name of the Lord." The music for gathering may be festive. Yet the shouts of Hosanna are under a shadow cast by the crucifixion to come. The service should embody the sharp contrasts of the week ahead. Indeed, it should enable the congregation to recognize the contrasts within the whole lenten journey which culminates in the mystery of

Christ's dying and rising. We encounter anew the ambiguity of our own participation in the triumphal entry and the passion of our Lord. Thus the music, which may include use of brass or other instruments, must reflect this range of theme. If the organ is used, the gathering place may be within hearing through the open doors of the church building. A choir is very helpful in the opening section of the service. Where a procession starts from a considerable distance, a short antiphon and response may be sung along the way by all.

Increasingly, congregations are exploring the following possibility: When weather and circumstances permit, the people gather outside, or in a hall or assembly room other than the sanctuary. At an appointed time the celebrant or other designated person welcomes the people and gives a brief introduction to the whole service. The various musical responses may be learned at this time, the palms distributed, and necessary instructions given. In this case the introduction precedes the responsory greeting, which should be sung if possible. This in turn may become the refrain sung in response to the proclamation of the entrance into Jerusalem and, if needed, in procession to the entrance of the church building where the hymn is begun.

If it is not possible to have a procession from outside the place of worship, the congregation may gather in the sanctuary and conduct the procession carrying palms, with the choir and perhaps a representative group of children and families. This may be easily done with such a group (or the whole congregation) moving around the outside aisles and back to their appointed seats, while the ministers and the choir move on into their places. In either case, palms or green branches should be distributed to all, and may be held and spontaneously waved during the entrance hymn.

In the second section of the service—the celebration of the Word of God—the focus is intensely on the proclamation of the Scriptures, principally the passion narrative appointed for the year. Particular care should be taken to help the people understand this aspect of worship, and to explore various ways in which the dramatic qualities of the Word may be brought to light.

Many persons have asked why the new calendar and lectionary—which United Methodists share with other historic Christian traditions—have combined Passion and Palm Sunday into one and have suggested such an extensive amount of Scripture. To understand why this has been done, one must first recognize that the passion story is a highly dramatic and unified whole and is absolutely central to each of the Gospels.[7] It demands to be heard in its wholeness, rather than in small bits and pieces. To focus upon this story one Sunday and then on the following Sunday to back up to the entry of Jesus into Jerusalem breaks the unity of the whole sweep of events from the triumphal entry through the passion and crucifixion to the resurrection.

There is also a pastoral reality to face. Most persons in church on Palm/Passion Sunday will not be there again until Easter Sunday. To go abruptly from the lesser joy of the entry into Jerusalem to the joy of Easter without being addressed by the passion and the cross of our Lord, is to impoverish our experience of the gospel. There is no crown and triumph without the suffering and the cross.

How can such a long passage of Scripture be included without unduly lenghthening the service and rendering it monotonous? It is essential to envision the telling of the story itself as a proclamation. There is no need to read the whole account and then to preach a full sermon as well. Here are four basic possibilities.

1. The Scripture can be read by the minister and other readers, with brief interpretive comments before, during, or following the reading. The presiding minister may also

retell the passion story in his or her own words; but this should be done only after extremely careful preparation. Of particular interest is *A Liturgical Interpretation of Our Lord's Passion in Narrative Form,* by John T. Townsend,[8] included in the service of Tenebrae later in this book, for both study and use. The reading of the passion may be accompanied by silent mime or by dramatization of certain key scenes by a group of players. Here as elsewhere, careful preparation and a well-disciplined and "understated" presentation is crucial.

2. More effectively, the passion account may be read or sung by lay persons. Specific roles are designated: narrator, Jesus, Pilate, the apostles, and other characters, and the crowd. As few as three persons are required if all the voices except the narrator and Jesus are spoken by one person. If members of the congregation are provided a text, or proper cues, they can take the role of the crowd. The choir may also take this role. In the following pages, texts from the three Synoptic Gospels are divided for easy dramatic presentation.

Positioning in the sanctuary is important. The narrator may use the pulpit, and the remaining readers may be clustered in groups at reading stands. Audibility is absolutely crucial. The readers should be well rehearsed and, where necessary, should be amplified. Microphones and electronic hardware should not, however, clutter the sanctuary. The movement as well as the positioning of the readers should be carefully planned.

3. The passion narrative may also be sung by the choir. While one of the traditional settings, such as J. S. Bach's, would be far too long, there are many shorter choral settings available. For a specific list of such music, write the Section on Worship, PO Box 840, Nashville, Tennessee 37202. Selections from the larger works may be woven together with dramatized readings as well. Advanced

planning and rehearsal are essential, as is wise choice in the level of difficulty of the music. It is better to offer something simple and well-done than something beyond the capacity of the choir.

4. Another possibility is a lessons-and-hymns pattern similar to the lessons and carols that many churches use at Christmas time for special services. Here are some suggestions for the three yearly cycles of readings:

Year A: Isaiah 50:4-9*a*

Sung Psalter (Psalm 22:1-11) or Anthem

Philippians 2:5-11

Hymn 74, 76, or 78

Matthew 26:14-29

Hymn 316, 413, or 170

Matthew 26:30-56

Hymn 237, 431, or 434

Matthew 26:57-75

Hymn 112, 412, or 418

Matthew 27:1-23

Hymn 112, 414, 415, 426, or 432

Matthew 27:24-50

Hymn 418, 420, or 429

Matthew 27:51-66

Hymn 428, 430, or 435

Year B: Zechariah 9:9-12

Sung Psalter (Psalm 22:7-8, 16-19, 22-23) or Anthem

Philippians 2:5-11

Hymn 74, 76, or 87

Mark 14:1-25

Hymn 316, 413, or 170

Mark 14:26-50

Hymn 237, 431, or 434

Mark 14:53-72

Hymn 112, 412, or 418
Mark 15:1-15
Hymn 112, 414, 415, 426, or 432
Mark 15:16-39
Hymn 418, 420, or 429
Mark 15:40-47
Hymn 428, 430, or 435

Year C: Deuteronomy 32:36-39
Sung Psalter (Psalm 31:1-5, 9-16) or Anthem
Philippians 2:5-11
Hymn 74, 76, or 78
Luke 22:14-30 or 14-23
Hymn 316, 413, or 170
Luke 22:31-62 or 39-48, 54-62
Hymn 327, 431, or 434
Luke 22:63–23:25 or 23:1-5, 13-25
Hymn 412, 418, or 173
Luke 23:26-43
Hymn 414, 415, or 417
Luke 23:44-56
Hymn 431, 435, or 436.

There will be a few situations when it may be necessary to preach a full sermon and to shorten the reading of the passion narrative. In this case a selected section upon which the sermon is based may be read. If this is done, it is strongly urged that the other portions of the story be read sometime during the next days of Holy Week. This may be possible on Sunday evening where evening services are the custom. Palm/Passion Sunday evening presents a number of possibilities, especially along the patterns developed above in 2 and 4. Note also the suggestions for using the passion narrative during Monday, Tuesday, and Wednesday services, mentioned in the next chapter. Other translations may, of course, be used, and will be divided according to the pattern that follows for each of the three years.

The Passion Narratives for the Three Years
Year A: 1981, 1984, 1987.

| Full form: | Matthew 26:14–27:66 |
| [Short form: | Matthew 27:11-54] |

The symbols in the margin represent the following: N–narrator, †–Christ, S–speakers other than Christ (these may be subdivided into male and female individual speakers, indicated by S_1, S_2, S_3, and Sps), C–the crowd.

N   Then one of the twelve, who was called Judas Iscariot, went to the chief priests and said,

S_1 "What will you give me if I deliver him to you?"

N   And they paid him thirty pieces of silver. And from that moment he sought an opportunity to betray him.

       Now on the first day of Unleavened Bread the disciples came to Jesus, saying,

Sps   "Where will you have us prepare for you to eat the passover?"

N   He said,

†   "Go into the city to such a one, and say to him, 'The Teacher says, My time is at hand; I will keep the passover at your house with my disciples.' "

N   And the disciples did as Jesus had directed them, and they prepared the passover.

       When it was evening, he sat at table with the twelve disciples; and as they were eating, he said,

†   "Truly, I say to you, one of you will betray me."

N   And they were very sorrowful, and began to say to him one after another,

S₂₍₃₎   "Is it I, Lord?" (*May be repeated.*)

N   He answered,

†   "He who has dipped his hand in the dish with me, will betray me. The Son of man goes as it is written of him, but woe to that man by whom the Son of man is betrayed! It would have been better for that man if he had not been born."

N   Judas, who betrayed him, said,

S₁   "Is it I, Master?"

N   He said to him,

†   "You have said so."

N   Now as they were eating, Jesus took bread, and blessed, and broke it, and gave it to the disciples and said,

†   "Take, eat; this is my body."

N   And he took a cup, and when he had given thanks he gave it to them, saying,

†   "Drink of it, all of you; for this is my blood of the covenant, which is poured out for many for the forgiveness of sins. I tell you I shall not drink again of this fruit of the vine until that day when I drink it new with you in my Father's kingdom."

N   And when they had sung a hymn, they went out to the Mount of Olives. Then Jesus said to them,

†   "You will all fall away because of me this night; for it is written, 'I will strike the shepherd, and the

sheep of the flock will be scattered.' But after I am raised up, I will go before you to Galilee.''

N   Peter declared to him,

S₂   "Though they all fall away because of you, I will never fall away."

N   Jesus said to him,

†   "Truly, I say to you, this very night, before the cock crows, you will deny me three times."

N   Peter said to him,

S₂   "Even if I must die with you, I will not deny you."

N   And so said all the disciples.
     Then Jesus went with them to a place called Gethsemane, and he said to his disciples,

†   "Sit here, while I go yonder and pray."

N   And taking with him Peter and the two sons of Zebedee, he began to be sorrowful and troubled. Then he said to them,

†   "My soul is very sorrowful, even to death; remain here, and watch with me."

N   And going a little farther he fell on his face and prayed,

†   "My Father, if it be possible, let this cup pass from me; nevertheless, not as I will, but as thou wilt."

N   And he came to the disciples and found them sleeping; and he said to Peter,

†   "So, could you not watch with me one hour? Watch and pray that you may not enter into

temptation; the spirit indeed is willing, but the flesh is weak."

N   Again, for the second time, he went away and prayed,

†   "My Father, if this cannot pass unless I drink it, thy will be done."

N   And again he came and found them sleeping, for their eyes were heavy. So, leaving them again, he went away and prayed for the third time, saying the same words. Then he came to the disciples and said to them,

†   "Are you still sleeping and taking your rest? Behold, the hour is at hand, and the Son of man is betrayed into the hands of sinners. Rise, let us be going; see, my betrayer is at hand."

N   While he was still speaking, Judas came, one of the twelve, and with him a great crowd with swords and clubs, from the chief priests and the elders of the people. Now the betrayer had given them a sign, saying,

S_1 "The one I shall kiss is the man; seize him."

N   And he came up to Jesus at once and said,

S_1 "Hail Master!"

N   And he kissed him. Jesus said to him,

†   "Friend, why are you here?"

N   Then they came up and laid hands on Jesus and seized him. And behold, one of those who were with Jesus stretched out his hand and drew his sword, and struck the slave of the high priest, and cut off his ear. Then Jesus said to him,

† "Put your sword back into its place; for all who take the sword will perish by the sword. Do you think that I cannot appeal to my Father, and he will at once send me more than twelve legions of angels? But how then should the scriptures be fulfilled, that it must be so?"

N At that hour Jesus said to the crowds,

† "Have you come out as against a robber, with swords and clubs to capture me? Day after day I sat in the temple teaching, and you did not seize me. But all this had taken place, that the scriptures of the prophets might be fulfilled."

N Then all the disciples forsook him and fled.
Then those who had seized Jesus led him to Caiaphas the high priest, where the scribes and the elders had gathered. But Peter followed him at a distance, as far as the courtyard of the high priest, and going inside he sat with the guards to see the end. Now the chief priests and the whole council sought false testimony against Jesus that they might put him to death, but they found none, though many false witnesses came forward. At last two came forward and said,

S₃ "This fellow said, 'I am able to destroy the temple of God, and to build it in three days.' "

N And the high priest stood up and said,

S₄ "Have you no answer to make? What is it that these men testify against you?"

N But Jesus was silent. And the high priest said to him,

S₄ "I adjure you by the living God, tell us if you are the Christ, the Son of God."

N Jesus said to him,

† "You have said so. But I tell you, hereafter you will see the Son of man seated at the right hand of Power, and coming on the clouds of heaven."

N Then the high priest tore his robes, and said,

S₄ "He has uttered blasphemy. Why do we still need witnesses? You have now heard his blasphemy. What is your judgment?"

N They answered,

C "He deserves death."

N Then they spat in his face, and struck him; and some slapped him, saying,

C "Prophesy to us, you Christ! Who is it that struck you?"

N Now Peter was sitting outside in the courtyard. And a maid came up to him, and said,

S₅ "You also were with Jesus the Galilean."

N But he denied it before them all, saying,

S₂ "I do not know what you mean."

N And when he went out to the porch, another maid saw him, and she said to the bystanders,

S₅ "This man was with Jesus of Nazareth."

N And again he denied it with an oath,

S₂ "I do not know the man."

N   After a little while the bystanders came up and said to Peter,

C   "Certainly you are also one of them, for your accent betrays you."

N   Then he began to invoke a curse on himself and to swear,

S_2 "I do not know the man."

N   And immediately the cock crowed. And Peter remembered the saying of Jesus, "Before the cock crows you will deny me three times." And he went out and wept bitterly.

        When morning came, all the chief priests and the elders of the people took counsel against Jesus to put him to death; and they bound him and led him away and delivered him to Pilate the governor.

        When Judas, his betrayer, saw that he was condemned, he repented and brought back the thirty pieces of silver to the chief priests and the elders, saying,

S_1 "I have sinned in betraying innocent blood."

N   They said,

Sps   "What is that to us? See to it yourself."

N   And throwing down the pieces of silver in the temple, he departed; and he went and hanged himself. But the chief priests, taking the pieces of silver, said,

Sps   "It is not lawful to put them into the treasury, since they are blood money."

N   So they took counsel, and bought with them the potter's field, to bury strangers in. Therefore that field has been called the Field of Blood to this day. Then was fulfilled what had been spoken by the prophet Jeremiah, saying, "And they took the thirty pieces of silver, the price of him on whom a price had been set by some of the sons of Israel, and they gave them for the potter's field, as the Lord directed me."

(Short form.)

[Now Jesus stood before the governor; and the governor asked him,

S₆   "Are you the King of the Jews?"

N   Jesus said to him,

†   "You have said so."

N   But when he was accused by the chief priests and elders, he made no answer. Then Pilate said to him,

S₆   "Do you not hear how many things they testify against you?"

N   But he gave no answer, not even to a single charge; so that the governor wondered greatly.

    Now at the feast the governor was accustomed to release for the crowd any one prisoner whom they wanted. And they had then a notorious prisoner, called Barabbas. So when they had gathered, Pilate said to them,

S₆   "Whom do you want me to release for you, Barabbas or Jesus who is called Christ?"

N   For he knew that it was out of envy that they had delivered him up. Besides, while he was sitting on the judgment seat, his wife sent word to him,

S₇   "Have nothing to do with that righteous man, for I have suffered much over him today in a dream."

N   Now the chief priests and the elders persuaded the people to ask for Barabbas and destroy Jesus. The governor again said to them,

S₆   "Which of the two do you want me to release for you?"

N   And they said,

C   "Barabbas."

N   Pilate said to them,

S₆   "Then what shall I do with Jesus who is called Christ?"

N   They all said,

C   "Let him be crucified."

N   And he said,

S₆   "Why, what evil has he done?"

N   But they shouted all the more,

C   "Let him be crucified!"

N   So when Pilate saw that he was gaining nothing, but rather that a riot was beginning, he took water and washed his hands before the crowd, saying,

S₆   "I an innocent of this man's blood; see to it yourselves."

N   Then he released for them Barabbas, and having scourged Jesus, delivered him to be crucified.
    Then the soldiers of the governor took Jesus into the praetorium, and they gathered the whole

battalion before him. And they stripped him and put a scarlet robe upon him, and plaiting a crown of thorns they put it on his head, and put a reed in his right hand. And kneeling before him they mocked him, saying,

C   "Hail, King of the Jews!"

N   And they spat upon him, and took the reed and struck him on the head. And when they had mocked him, they stripped him of the robe, and put his own clothes on him, and led him away to crucify him.

     As they went out, they came upon a man of Cyrene, Simon by name; this man they compelled to carry his cross. And when they came to a place called Golgotha (which means the place of a skull), they offered him wine to drink, mingled with gall; but when he tasted it, he would not drink it. And when they had crucified him, they divided his garments among them by casting lots; then they sat down and kept watch over him there. And over his head they put the charge against him, which read, "This is Jesus the King of the Jews." Then two robbers were crucified with him, one on the right and one on the left. And those who passed by derided him, wagging their heads and saying,

C   "You who would destroy the temple and build it in three days, save yourself! If you are the Son of God, come down from the cross."

N   So also the chief priests, with the scribes and elders, mocked him, saying,

Sps   "He saved others; he cannot save himself. He is the king of Israel; let him come down now from the cross, and we will believe in him. He trusts in God; let God deliver him now, if he desires him; for he said, 'I am the Son of God.' "

N And the robbers who were crucified with him also reviled him in the same way.

   Now from the sixth hour there was darkness over all the land until the ninth hour. And about the ninth hour Jesus cried with a loud voice,

† "Eli, Eli, lama sabach-tha'ni?"

N that is,

† "My God, my God, why hast thou forsaken me?"

N And some of the bystanders hearing it said,

Sps "This man is calling Elijah."

N And one of them at once ran and took a sponge, filled it with vinegar, and put it on a reed, and gave it to him to drink. But the others said,

Sps "Wait, let us see whether Elijah will come to save him."

N And Jesus cried again with a loud voice and yielded up his spirit.

(A brief pause.)

  And behold, the curtain of the temple was torn in two, from top to bottom; and the earth shook, and the rocks were split; the tombs also were opened, and many bodies of the saints who had fallen asleep were raised, and coming out of the tombs after his resurrection they went into the holy city and appeared to many. When the centurion and those who were with him, keeping watch over

Jesus, saw the earthquake and what took place, they were filled with awe, and said,

Sps   "Truly this was the Son of God!"]

(Short form ends.)

N   There were also many women there, looking on from afar, who had followed Jesus from Galilee, ministering to him; among whom were Mary Magdalene, and Mary the mother of James and Joseph, and the mother of the sons of Zebedee.

When it was evening, there came a rich man from Arimathea, named Joseph, who also was a disciple of Jesus. He went to Pilate and asked for the body of Jesus. Then Pilate ordered it to be given to him. And Joseph took the body, and wrapped it in a clean linen shroud, and laid it in his own new tomb, which he had hewn in the rock; and he rolled a great stone to the door of the tomb, and departed. Mary Magdalene and the other Mary were there, sitting opposite the sepulchre.

Next day, that is, after the day of Preparation, the chief priests and the Pharisees gathered before Pilate and said,

Sps   "Sir, we remember how that imposter said, while he was still alive, 'After three days I will rise again.' Therefore order the sepulchre to be made secure until the third day, lest his disciples go and steal him away, and tell the people, 'He has risen from the dead,' and the last fraud will be worse than the first."

N   Pilate said to them,

S$_6$ "You have a guard of soldiers; go, make it as secure as you can."

N   So they went and made the sepulchre secure by sealing the stone and setting a guard.

⁣   *⁣*   *⁣*

Year B: 1979, 1982, 1985.
    Full form: Mark 14:1–15:47
    [Short form: Mark 15:1-39]
    The symbols in the margin represent the following: N–narrator; †–Christ; S–speakers other than Christ (these may be subdivided into male and female individual speakers, indicated by S_1, S_2, S_3, and Sps); C–the crowd.

N   It was now two days before the Passover and the feast of Unleavened Bread. And the chief priests and the scribes were seeking how to arrest him by stealth, and kill him; for they said,

Sps   "Not during the feast, lest there be a tumult of the people."

N   And while he was at Bethany in the house of Simon the leper, as he sat at table, a woman came with an alabaster flask of ointment of pure nard, very costly, and she broke the flask and poured it over his head. But there were some who said to themselves indignantly,

Sps   "Why was the ointment thus wasted? For this ointment might have been sold for more than three hundred denarii, and given to the poor."

N   And they reproached her. But Jesus said,

†   "Let her alone; why do you trouble her? She has done a beautiful thing to me. For you always have the poor with you, and whenever you will, you can do good to them; but you will not always have me.

76

She has done what she could; she has anointed my body beforehand for burying. And truly, I say to you, wherever the gospel is preached in the whole world, what she has done will be told in memory of her."

N   Then Judas Iscariot, who was one of the twelve, went to the chief priests in order to betray him to them. And when they heard it they were glad, and promised to give him money. And he sought an opportunity to betray him.

And on the first day of Unleavened Bread, when they sacrificed the passover lamb, his disciples said to him,

Sps   "Where will you have us go and prepare for you to eat the passover?"

N   And he sent two of his disciples, and said to them,

†   "Go into the city, and a man carrying a jar of water will meet you; follow him, and wherever he enters, say to the householder, 'The Teacher says, Where is my guest room, where I am to eat the passover with my disciples?' And he will show you a large upper room furnished and ready; there prepare for us."

N   And the disciples set out and went to the city, and found it as he had told them; and they prepared the passover.

And when it was evening he came with the twelve. And as they were at table eating, Jesus said,

†   "Truly, I say to you, one of you will betray me, one who is eating with me."

N   They began to be sorrowful, and to say to him one after another,

Sps   "Is it I?" *(May be repeated.)*

N   He said to them,

†   "It is one of the twelve, one who is dipping bread in the same dish with me. For the Son of man goes as it is written of him, but woe to that man by whom the Son of man is betrayed! It would have been better for that man if he had not been born."

N   And as they were eating, he took bread, and blessed, and broke it, and gave it to them, and said,

†   "Take; this is my body."

N   And he took a cup, and when he had given thanks he gave it to them, and they all drank of it. And he said to them,

†   "This is my blood of the covenant, which is poured out for many. Truly, I say to you, I shall not drink again of the fruit of the vine until that day when I drink it new in the kingdom of God."

N   And when they had sung a hymn, they went out to the Mount of Olives. And Jesus said to them,

†   "You will all fall away; for it is written, 'I will strike the shepherd, and the sheep will be scattered.' But after I am raised up, I will go before you to Galilee."

N   Peter said to him,

S_1 "Even though they all fall away, I will not."

N   And Jesus said to him,

†   "Truly, I say to you, this very night, before the cock crows twice, you will deny me three times."

N   But he said vehemently,

S_1 "If I must die with you, I will not deny you."

N   And they all said the same.
    And they went to a place which was called Gethsemane; and he said to his disciples,

†   "Sit here, while I pray."

N   And he took with him Peter and James and John, and began to be greatly distressed and troubled. And he said to them,

†   "My soul is very sorrowful, even to death; remain here, and watch."

N   And going a little farther he fell on the ground and prayed that, if it were possible, the hour might pass from him. And he said,

†   "Abba, Father, all things are possible to thee; remove this cup from me; yet not what I will, but what thou wilt."

N   And he came and found them sleeping, and he said to Peter,

†   "Simon, are you asleep? Could you not watch one hour? Watch and pray that you may not enter into temptation; The spirit indeed is willing, but the flesh is weak."

N   And again he went away and prayed, saying the same words. And again he came and found them sleeping, for their eyes were very heavy; and they did not know what to answer him. And he came the third time, and said to them,

†   "Are you still sleeping and taking your rest? It is enough; the hour has come; the Son of man is betrayed into the hands of sinners. Rise, let us be going; see, my betrayer is at hand."

N   And immediately, while he was still speaking, Judas came, one of the twelve, and with him a crowd with swords and clubs, from the chief priests and the scribes and the elders. Now the betrayer had given them a sign, saying,

S_2 "The one I shall kiss is the man; seize him and lead him away under guard."

N   And when he came, he went up to him at once, and said,

S_2 "Master!"

N   And he kissed him. And they laid hands on him and seized him. But one of those who stood by drew his sword, and struck the slave of the high priest and cut off his ear. And Jesus said to them,

†   "Have you come out as against a robber, with swords and clubs to capture me? Day after day I was with you in the temple teaching, and you did not seize me. But let the scriptures be fulfilled."

N   And they all forsook him, and fled.

    And a young man followed him, with nothing but a linen cloth about his body; and they seized him, but he left the linen cloth and ran away naked.

    And they led Jesus to the high priest; and all the chief priests and the elders and the scribes were assembled. And Peter had followed him at a distance, right into the courtyard of the high priest; and he was sitting with the guards, and warming himself at the fire. Now the chief priests and the whole council sought testimony against Jesus to put him to death; but they found none. For many bore false witness against him, and their witness did not agree. And some stood up and bore false witness against him, saying,

Sps   "We heard him say, 'I will destroy this temple that is made with hands, and in three days I will build another, not made with hands.' "

N   Yet not even so did their testimony agree. And the high priest stood up in the midst, and asked Jesus,

S₃   "Have you no answer to make? What is it that these men testify against you?"

N   But he was silent and made no answer. Again the high priest asked him,

S₃   "Are you the Christ, the Son of the Blessed?"

N   And Jesus said,

†   "I am; and you will see the Son of man seated at the right hand of Power, and coming with the clouds of heaven."

N   And the high priest tore his garments, and said,

S₃   "Why do we still need witnesses? You have heard his blasphemy, What is your decision?"

N   And they all condemned him as deserving death. And some began to spit on him, and to cover his face, and to strike him, saying to him,

Sps   "Prophesy!"

N   And the guards received him with blows.
      And as Peter was below in the courtyard, one of

the maids of the high priest came; and seeing Peter warming himself, she looked at him, and said,

S₄   "You also were with the Nazarene, Jesus."

N   But he denied it, saying,

S₁   "I neither know nor understand what you mean."

N   And he went out in to the gateway. And the maid saw him, and began again to say to the bystanders,

S₄   "This man is one of them."

N   But again he denied it. And after a little while again the bystanders said to Peter,

Sps   "Certainly you are one of them; for you are a Galilean."

N   But he began to invoke a curse on himself and to swear,

S₁   "I do not know this man of whom you speak."

N   And immediately the cock crowed a second time. And Peter remembered how Jesus had said to him, "Before the cock crows twice, you will deny me three times." And he broke down and wept.

(Short form.)

[And as soon as it was morning the chief priests, with the elders and scribes, and the whole council held a consultation; and they bound Jesus and led him away and delivered him to Pilate. And Pilate asked him,

S₅   "Are you the King of the Jews?"

N   And he answered him,

†   "You have said so."

N   And the chief priests accused him of many things. And Pilate again asked him,

S₅   "Have you no answer to make? See how many charges they bring against you."

N   But Jesus made no further answer, so that Pilate wondered.

      Now at the feast he used to release for them one prisoner for whom they asked. And among the rebels in prison, who had committed murder in the insurrection, there was a man called Barabbas. And the crowd came up and began to ask Pilate to do as he was wont to do for them. And he answered them,

S₅   "Do you want me to release for you the King of the Jews?"

N   For he perceived that it was out of envy that the chief priests had delivered him up. But the chief priests stirred up the crowd to have him release for them Barabbas instead. And Pilate again said to them,

S₅   "Then what shall I do with the man whom you call the King of the Jews?"

N   And they cried out again,

C   "Crucify him."

N   So Pilate, wishing to satisfy the crowd, released for them Barabbas; and having scourged Jesus, he delivered him to be crucified.

      And the soldiers led him away inside the palace (that is, the praetorium); and they called together the whole battalion. And they clothed him in a purple cloak, and plaiting a crown of thorns they put it on him. And they began to salute him,

Sps   "Hail, King of the Jews!"

N   And they struck his head with a reed, and spat upon him, and they knelt down in homage to him. And when they had mocked him, they stripped him of the purple cloak, and put his own clothes on him. And they led him out to crucify him.

And they compelled a passer-by, Simon of Cyrene, who was coming in from the country, the father of Alexander and Rufus, to carry his cross. And they brought him to the place called Golgotha (which means the place of a skull). And they offered him wine mingled with myrrh; but he did not take it. And they crucified him, and divided his garments among them, casting lots for them, to decide what each should take. And it was the third hour, when they crucified him. And the inscription of the charge against him read, "The King of the Jews." And with him they crucified two robbers, one on his right and one on his left. And those who passed by derided him, wagging their heads, and saying,

C   "Aha! You who would destroy the temple and build it in three days, save yourself, and come down from the cross!"

N   So also the chief priests mocked him to one another with the scribes, saying,

Sps   "He saved others; he cannot save himself. Let the Christ, the King of Israel, come down now from the cross, that we may see and believe."

N   Those who were crucified with him also reviled him.

      And when the sixth hour had come, there was darkness over the whole land until the ninth hour. And at the ninth hour Jesus cried with a loud voice,

†   "Eloi, Eloi, lama sabach-tha'ni?"

N   which means

†   "My God, my God, why hast thou forsaken me?"

N   And some of the bystanders hearing it said,

Sps   "Behold, he is calling Elijah."

N   And one ran and, filling a sponge full of vinegar, put it on a reed and gave it to him to drink, saying,

S₆   "Wait, let us see whether Elijah will come to take him down."

N   And Jesus uttered a loud cry, and breathed his last. And the curtain of the temple was torn in two, from top to bottom. And when the centurion, who stood facing him, saw that he thus breathed his last, he said,

S₇   "Truly this man was the Son of God!"]

(Short form ends.)

N   There were also women looking on from afar, among whom were Mary Magdalene, and Mary the mother of James the younger and of Joses, and Salome, who, when he was in Galilee, followed him, and ministered to him; and also many other women who came up with him to Jerusalem.

      And when evening had come, since it was the day of Preparation, that is, the day before the sabbath, Joseph of Arimathea, a respected member of the council, who was also himself looking for the kingdom of God, took courage and went to Pilate, and asked for the body of Jesus. And Pilate wondered if he were already dead; and summoning the centurion, he asked him whether he was already dead. And when he learned from the centurion that he was dead, he granted the body to Joseph. And he bought a linen shroud, and taking him down, wrapped him in the linen shroud, and laid him in a tomb which had been hewn out of the rock; and he rolled a stone against the door of the tomb. Mary Magadalene and Mary the mother of Joses saw where he was laid.

*
**   *
**   *
**

Year C: 1980, 1983, 1986
>Full form: Luke 22:14–23:56
>[Short form: Luke 23:1-49]
>*The symbols in the margin represent the following: N–narrator; †–Christ; S–speakers other than Christ (these may be subdivided into male and female individual speakers, indicated by S_1, S_2, S_3, and Sps); C–the crowd.*

N   And when the hour came, he sat at table, and the apostles with him. And he said to them,

†   "I have earnestly desired to eat this passover with you before I suffer; for I tell you I shall not eat it until it is fulfilled in the kingdom of God."

N   And he took a cup, and when he had given thanks he said,

†   "Take this, and divide it among yourselves; for I tell you that from now on I shall not drink of the fruit of the vine until the kingdom of God comes."

N   And he took bread, and when he had given thanks he broke it and gave it to them, saying,

†   "This is my body. But behold the hand of him who betrays me is with me on the table. For the Son of man goes as it has been determined; but woe to that man by whom he is betrayed!"

N   And they began to question one another, which of them it was that would do this.

A dispute also arose among them, which of them was to be regarded as the greatest. And he said to them,

†   "The kings of the Gentiles exercise lordship over them; and those in authority over them are called benefactors. But not so with you; rather let the greatest among you become as the youngest, and the leader as one who serves. For which is the greater one, who sits at table, or one who serves? Is it not the one who sits at table? But I am among you as one who serves.

"You are those who have continued with me in my trials; and I assign to you, as my Father assigned to me a kingdom, that you may eat and drink at my table in my kingdom, and sit on thrones judging the twelve tribes of Israel.

"Simon, Simon, behold, Satan demanded to have you, that he might sift you like wheat, but I have prayed for you that your faith may not fail; and when you have turned again, strengthen your brethren."

N   And he said to him,

S_1 "Lord, I am ready to go with you to prison and to death."

N He said,

† "I tell you, Peter, the cock will not crow this day, until you three times deny that you know me."

N And he said to them,

† "When I sent you out with no purse or bag or sandals, did you lack anything?"

N They said,

Sps "Nothing."

N He said to them,

† "But now, let him who has a purse take it, and likewise a bag. And let him who has no sword sell his mantle and buy one. For I tell you that this scripture must be fulfilled in me, 'And he was reckoned with transgressors'; for what is written about me has its fulfillment."

N And they said,

Sps "Look, Lord, here are two swords."

N And he said to them,

† "It is enough."

N And he came out, and went, as was his custom, to the Mount of Olives; and the disciples followed him. And when he came to the place he said to them,

† "Pray that you may not enter into temptation."

N And he withdrew from them about a stone's throw, and knelt down and prayed,

† "Father, if thou art willing, remove this cup from me; nevertheless not my will, but thine, be done."

N   And when he rose from prayer, he came to the disciples and found them sleeping for sorrow, and he said to them,

†   "Why do you sleep? Rise and pray that you may not enter into temptation."

N   While he was still speaking, there came a crowd, and the man called Judas, one of the twelve, was leading them. He drew near to Jesus to kiss him; but Jesus said to him,

†   "Judas, would you betray the Son of man with a kiss?"

N   And when those who were about him saw what would follow, they said,

Sps   "Lord, shall we strike with the sword?"

N   And one of them struck the slave of the high priest and cut off his right ear. But Jesus said,

†   "No more of this!"

N   And he touched his ear and healed him. Then Jesus said to the chief priests and officers of the temple and elders, who had come out against him,

†   "Have you come out as against a robber, with swords and clubs? When I was with you day after day in the temple, you did not lay hands on me. But this is your hour, and the power of darkness."

N   Then they seized him and led him away, bringing him into the high priest's house. Peter followed at a distance; and when they had kindled a fire in the middle of the courtyard and sat down together, Peter sat among them. Then a maid, seeing him as he sat in the light and gazing at him, said,

S₂   "This man also was with him."

N   But he denied it, saying,

S₁   "Woman, I do not know him."

N   And a little later some one else saw him and said,

S₃   "You also are one of them."

N   But Peter said,

S₁   "Man, I am not."

N   And after an interval of about an hour still another insisted, saying,

S₄   "Certainly this man also was with him; for he is a Galilean."

N   But Peter said,

S₁   "Man, I do not know what you are saying."

N   And immediately, while he was still speaking, the cock crowed. And the Lord turned and looked at Peter. And Peter remembered the word of the Lord, how he had said to him, "Before the cock crows today, you will deny me three times." And he went out and wept bitterly.

     Now the men who were holding Jesus mocked him and beat him; they also blindfolded him and asked him,

Sps   "Prophesy! Who is it that struck you?"

N   And they spoke many other words against him, reviling him.

     When day came, the assembly of the elders of the people gathered together, both chief priests and scribes; and they led him away to their council, and they said,

Sps   "If you are the Christ, tell us."

N   But he said to them,

†   "If I tell you, you will not believe; and if I ask you, you will not answer. But from now on the Son of man shall be seated at the right hand of the power of God."

N   And they all said,

Sps   "Are you the Son of God, then?"

N   And he said to them,

†   "You say that I am."

N   And they said,

Sps   "What further testimony do we need? We have heard it ourselves from his own lips."

(Short form.)

N   [Then the whole company of them arose, and brought him before Pilate. And they began to accuse him, saying,

Sps   "We found this man perverting our nation, and forbidding us to give tribute to Caesar, and saying that he himself is Christ a king."

N   And Pilate asked him,

S_5 "Are you the King of the Jews?"

N   And he answered him,

†   "You have said so."

N   And Pilate said to the chief priests and the multitudes,

S_5 "I find no crime in this man."

N   But they were urgent, saying,

Sps   "He stirs up the people, teaching throughout all Judea, from Galilee even to this place."

N   When Pilate heard this, he asked whether the man was a Galilean. And when he learned that he belonged to Herod's jurisdiction, he sent him over to Herod, who was himself in Jerusalem at that time. When Herod saw Jesus, he was very glad, for he had long desired to see him, because he had heard about him, and he was hoping to see some sign done by him. So he questioned him at some length; but he made no answer. The chief priests and the scribes stood by, vehemently accusing him. And Herod with his soldiers treated him with contempt and mocked him, then, arraying him in gorgeous apparel, he sent him back to Pilate. And Herod and Pilate became friends with each other that very day, for before this they had been at enmity with each other.

    Pilate then called together the chief priests and the rulers and the people, and said to them.

S₅   "You brought me this man as one who was perverting the people; and after examining him before you, behold, I did not find this man guilty of any of your charges against him; neither did Herod, for he sent him back to us. Behold, nothing deserving death has been done by him; I will therefore chastise him and release him."

N   But they all cried out together,

C   "Away with this man, and release to us Barabbas"—

N   a man who had been thrown into prison for an insurrection started in the city, and for murder.

Pilate addressed them once more, desiring to release Jesus; but they shouted out,

C   "Crucify, crucify him!"

N   A third time he said to them,

S₅   "Why, what evil has he done? I have found in him no crime deserving death; I will therefore chastise him and release him."

N   But they were urgent, demanding with loud cries that he should be crucified. And their voices prevailed. So Pilate gave sentence that their demand should be granted. He released the man who had been thrown into prison for insurrection and murder, whom they asked for; but Jesus he delivered up to their will.

And as they led him away, they seized one Simon of Cyrene, who was coming in from the country, and laid on him the cross, to carry it behind Jesus. And there followed him a great multitude of the people, and of women who bewailed and lamented him. But Jesus turning to them, said,

†   "Daughters of Jerusalem, do not weep for me, but weep for yourselves and for your children. For behold, the days are coming when they will say, 'Blessed are the barren, and the wombs that never bore, and the breasts that never gave suck!' Then they will begin to say to the mountains, 'Fall on us'; and to the hills, 'Cover us.' For if they do this when the wood is green, what will happen when it is dry?"

N   Two others also, who were criminals, were led away to be put to death with him. And when they came to the place which is called The Skull, there they crucified him, and the criminals, one on the right and one on the left. And Jesus said,

† ,"Father, forgive them; for they know not what they do."

N And they cast lots to divide his garments. And the people stood by, watching; but the rulers scoffed at him, saying,

Sps "He saved others; let him save himself, if he is the Christ of God, his Chosen One!"

N The soldiers also mocked him, coming up and offering him vinegar, and saying,

Sps "If you are the King of the Jews, save yourself!"

N There was also an inscription over him, "This is the King of the Jews."

One of the criminals who were hanged railed at him, saying,

S_6 "Are you not the Christ? Save yourself and us!"

N But the other rebuked him, saying,

S_7 "Do you not fear God, since you are under the same sentence of condemnation? And we indeed justly; for we are receiving the due reward of our deeds; but this man has done nothing wrong."

N And he said,

S_7 "Jesus, remember me when you come into your kingdom."

N And he said to him,

† "Truly, I say to you, today you will be with me in Paradise."

N   It was now about the sixth hour, and there was darkness over the whole land until the ninth hour, while the sun's light failed; and the curtain of the temple was torn in two. Then Jesus, crying with a loud voice, said,

†   "Father, into thy hands I commit my spirit!"

N   And having said this he breathed his last. Now when the centurion saw what had taken place, he praised God, and said,

S₈   "Certainly this man was innocent!"

N   And all the multitudes who assembled to see the sight, when they saw what had taken place, returned home beating their breasts. And all his acquaintances and the women who had followed him from Galilee stood at a distance and saw these things.]

(Short form ends.)

Now there was a man named Joseph from the Jewish town of Arimathea. He was a member of the council, a good and righteous man, who had not consented to their purpose and deed, and he was looking for the kingdom of God. This man went to Pilate and asked for the body of Jesus. Then he took it down and wrapped it in a linen shroud, and laid him in a rock-hewn tomb, where no one had ever yet been laid. It was the day of Preparation, and the sabbath was beginning. The women who had come with him from Galilee followed, and saw the tomb, and how his body was laid; then they returned, and prepared spices and ointments.

On the sabbath they rested according to the commandment.

V.

Monday, Tuesday, and Wednesday of Holy Week: Orders of Worship with Commentary

Monday

GATHERING   *Suitable music may be offered.*

GREETING

Grace and peace from God our Father
and the Lord Jesus Christ.

Amen.

Come, let us worship the Lord,
who was obedient even unto death on a cross.

We come in spirit and in truth.

HYMN   *See* The Book of Hymns, *412-22, 426-36.*

OPENING PRAYER
The Lord be with you.

And also with you.

Let us pray: *A brief silence.*

God of strength and mercy,
by the suffering and death of your Son,
free us from slavery to sin and death
and protect us in all our weakness;
Through Jesus Christ our Lord. Amen.

FIRST LECTION   Isaiah 42:1-6   (Years A,B,C)

PSALM or ANTHEM   Psalm 36:5-10
Antiphon: **How priceless is your love, O God!**
Your love, O Lord, reaches to the heavens,
and your faithfulness to the clouds.

Your righteousness is like the strong mountains
your justice like the great deep;
you save both man and beast, O Lord.

How priceless is your love, O God!
your people take refuge under the shadow of your
wings.

They feast upon the abundance of your house;
you give them drink from the river of your delights.

For with you is the well of life,
and in your light we see light.

Continue your loving-kindness to those who know
you,
and your favor to those who are true of heart.
Antiphon: **How priceless is your love, O God!**

SECOND LECTION   Hebrews 9:11-15   (Years
A,B,C)

RESPONSORY
Now is the acceptable time.

Now is the time of salvation.

Let us prove ourselves in patience,
in the power of the Lord.

**Now is the acceptable time,
Now is the time of salvation.**

Let us live as God's servants
watching in the word of truth,
in the power of redeeming love.

**Now is the season of hope,
Now is the acceptable time,
Now is the day of salvation near.**

THE GOSPEL   John 12:1-11   (Years A,B,C)

MEDITATION   *Silent, or other; see commentary.*

INTERCESSIONS

In peace, let us pray to the Lord:

The people respond. **Lord, have mercy,** *or*
Hear us in your mercy.

For the unity, peace and welfare of the church
   and for all our sisters and brothers in Christ,
   let us pray to the Lord.

For all ministers of the gospel who speak the truth in
   love,
   let us pray to the Lord.

For all prophets of justice, and those who bring mercy,
   and for all who serve and defend human life,
   let us pray to the Lord.

For the destruction of demonic powers,
   the elimination of slavery, human exploitation, and
   war,
   let us pray to the Lord.

Spontaneous petitions may be added.

Help, save, pity, and defend us, O God, by your grace.

A brief silence is kept.

Rejoicing in the fellowship of all the saints,
    let us commend ourselves, one another
    and the whole world to Christ our Lord.

To you, O Lord.

[COLLECT   *The following may be used between the
            intercessions and the Lord's Prayer.*

Almighty God,
    whose dear Son went not up to joy
    before he suffered pain,
    and entered not into glory before he was crucified:
Mercifully grant that we,
    walking in the way of the cross,
    may find it the way of life and peace;
Through Jesus Christ your Son our Lord,
    who lives and reigns with you and the Holy Spirit,
    one God, for ever. **Amen.**]

THE LORD'S PRAYER

HYMN

DISMISSAL WITH BLESSING
    Go forth in peace to walk the way of life.

We go in the name of the Lord.

Now may the God of peace who brought again from the
    dead
Our Lord Jesus, the great shepherd of the sheep,
by the blood of the eternal covenant,
equip you with everything good that you may do his will,
working in you that which is pleasing in his sight,
through Jesus Christ; to whom be glory for ever and ever.

Amen. Thanks be to God.

The hymn may be used following the dismissal with blessing, the congregation departing quietly so that some may remain for meditation.

Tuesday

GATHERING   *Suitable music may be offered.*

GREETING

Grace and peace from the Lord Jesus Christ be with you all.

And also with you.

Come, let us worship the Lord,
who was obedient even unto death on a cross.

We come in spirit and in truth.

HYMN

OPENING PRAYER
Let us pray: *A brief silence.*

God of strength and mercy,
  By the passion of your blessed Son
  you made an instrument of shameful death
  to be for us the means of life:
Grant us so to glory in the cross of Christ,
  that we may gladly suffer shame and loss
  for the sake of Jesus Christ our Savior;
Through whom in the Holy Spirit we pray. Amen.

FIRST LECTION   Isaiah 49:1-9*a*   (Years A,B,C)

PSALM   Psalm 71:1-12, 15, 17
          Antiphon: **I will sing of your salvation.**

100

In you, O Lord, have I taken refuge;
  let me never be ashamed.
In your righteousness, deliver me and set me free;
  incline your ear to me and save me.

Antiphon

Be my strong rock, a castle to keep me safe;
  you are my crag and my stronghold.
Deliver me, my God, from the hand of the wicked,
  from the clutches of the evildoer and the oppressor.

Antiphon

For you are my hope, O Lord God,
  my confidence since I was young.
I have been sustained by you ever since I was born;
  from my mother's womb you have been my strength;
  my praise shall be always of you.

Antiphon

I have become a portent to many;
  but you are my refuge and my strength.
Let my mouth be full of your praise
  and your glory all the day long.
Do not cast me off in my old age;
  forsake me not when my strength fails.
For my enemies are talking against me,
  and those who lie in wait for my life take counsel
  together.

Antiphon

They say, "God has forsaken him;
go after him and seize him;
  because there is none who will save."
O God, be not far from me;
  come quickly to help me, O my God.
My mouth shall recount your mighty acts
and saving deeds all day long;
  though I cannot know the number of them.

O God, you have taught me since I was young,
and to this day I tell of your wonderful works.
Antiphon: **I will sing of your salvation.**

SECOND LECTION   I Corinthians 1:18-31
(Years A,B,C)

RESPONSORY
Let us glory in the cross of Jesus Christ.
Through him we have salvation,
life and resurrection.

Cross of Christ, tree of hope.

For us he became obedient even to death on a cross;
because of this God exalted him above every name.

Cross of Christ, tree of hope,
Wisdom of God.

When I am lifted up from the earth,
I will draw all unto myself.

Cross of Christ, tree of hope, wisdom of God.
We worship and praise you, O Christ;
by your cross the world is redeemed.

THE GOSPEL   John 12:37-50   (Years A,B,C)

MEDITATION   *Silent, or other; see commentary.*

INTERCESSIONS   *See pages 98-99.*

[COLLECT]   *See page 99.*

THE LORD'S PRAYER

HYMN

DISMISSAL WITH BLESSING
Go forth to walk the way of the cross;
May God bless and keep you in his mercy.

We go in the name of the Lord.

Now to him who by the power at work within us
is able to do far more abundantly than all we ask or think
to him be glory in the church
and in Christ Jesus to all generations,
for ever and ever.

Amen. Thanks be to God.

*The hymn may be sung following the dismissal with
blessing, the congregation departing quietly so that some
may remain for meditation.*

Wednesday

GATHERING   *Suitable music may be offered.*

GREETING
  Grace and peace from God our Father
  and the Lord Jesus Christ.

  Amen.

  Come, let us worship the Lord,
  who was obedient even unto death on a cross.

  We come in spirit and in truth.

HYMN   *See* The Book of Hymns, *412-22, 426-36.*

OPENING PRAYER
  The Lord be with you.

  And also with you.

  Let us pray: *A brief silence.*
  Most merciful God,
    whose blessed Son our Savior was betrayed, whipped,
    and his face spat upon:

Grant us grace to take joyfully
   the sufferings of the present time,
   confident of the glory that shall yet be revealed;
Through Jesus Christ our Lord,
   who lives and reigns with you and the Holy Spirit,
   one God, for ever and ever. **Amen.**

FIRST LECTION   Isaiah 50:4-9   (Years A,B,C)

PSALM OR ANTHEM   Psalm 70:1-2, 4-5
   Antiphon: **O Lord, make haste to help me.**
Be pleased, O God, to deliver me;
   O Lord, make haste to help me.
Let those who seek my life be ashamed
and altogether dismayed;
   let those who take pleasure in my misfortune
   draw back and be disgraced.
Let all who seek you rejoice and be glad in you;
   let those who love your salvation say for ever,
   "Great is the Lord!"
But as for me, I am poor and needy!
   come to me speedily, O God.
   Antiphon: **O Lord, make haste to help me.**

SECOND LECTION Romans 5:6-11 (Years A,B,C)

RESPONSORY
Now is the acceptable time.

Now is the time of salvation.

Since we are justified by grace through faith,
we have peace with God through our Lord Jesus Christ.
Now is the acceptable time.
Now is the time of salvation.

Let us rejoice in our hope and our sufferings.
For this hope does not disappoint us,

104

since God's love has been poured into our hearts
through the Holy Spirit.

**Now is the season of hope,
Now is the acceptable time,
Now is the day of salvation near.**

THE GOSPEL   John 13:21-38   (Years A,B,C)

MEDITATION   *Silent, or other; see commentary.*

INTERCESSIONS   *See pages 98-99.*

[COLLECT]   *See page 99.*

THE LORD'S PRAYER

HYMN

DISMISSAL WITH BLESSING
Go forth in peace to walk the way of his suffering.

We go in the name of the Lord.

May the God of peace enable us to do his will
in every kind of goodness,
working in us what pleases him
in the Holy Spirit;
through Jesus Christ our Lord.

Amen. Thanks be to God.

Commentary

On Palm/Passion Sunday the whole congregation has
gathered to recall and to celebrate the dramatic beginning
of these days of the passion and death of our Lord. It begins
the period of time traditionally known as Holy Week.
These are among the most intense days in the church's year
of grace, culminating in the Easter Triduum (Thursday
sunset to Sunday sunset). We here approach the yearly

renewal of our incorporation into the central mystery of Christian life and faith.

Monday through Thursday afternoon comprises the minor days of Holy Week, but nonetheless they are occasions for dwelling together upon Scripture, particularly the portrayal of the final events, and for pondering their meaning for us in the context of prayer and meditation. Note that a service has not been provided for Thursday; but if one is needed, the same pattern as for the first three days may be followed. While many churches cannot expect most of the congregation to gather each of these days, increasingly we find the need for services that may be held in church buildings or in homes. In many communities, there is a well-established tradition of noonday worship, often of an ecumenical nature; many others hold brief early evening services for which these resources are appropriate.

The order and texts of these services are designed for communal gatherings in a church building; but with some adaptation they are suitable for family use as well. The psalms, prayers, and various responsories are integrated with the readings from Scripture, and are extensions of the Holy Week themes. The meditative style and tone of these services should be preserved in the hymn selection and in other musical elements, such as choral settings. This is especially important in a congregational setting. Careful choice in light of the themes and images found in the Word of God is required.

In some cases the psalms may be sung by the choir, the congregation responding with the antiphons; or the congregation may sing or recite the whole psalm in sections (see chapter 2 for further suggestions). Pastors and church musicians should discuss the use of existing choral literature that may be adaptable to congregational participations. Of course, in some circumstances, having no music may be effective and in keeping with the austerity of the time and the setting.

Several persons may be involved in leading these services: readers, leaders of prayer, musicians, acolytes, book-bearers, and the presiding ministers. On ecumenical occasions, several denominations can thus take part. Lay involvement is to be encouraged whenever possible. Adequate preparation of the participants is essential. Since these are primarily meditative services, a solemnity and reserve coupled wih pastoral grace is desirable. A spirit of communal prayer should be present.

There are a variety of ways in which Scripture may be incorporated. If for some reason the full passion narrative was not proclaimed on Sunday, selections from the synoptic account for the particular year may be read or enacted in addition to, or in the place of, the Johannine readings which are indicated. Nonbiblical readings may also be used as a commentary and as response to the Scripture, if a slightly longer service is possible. They would normally last twenty-five to thirty minutes.

In many instances music, both instrumental and vocal, may play a significant part. It should always be kept in mind that these services prepare us for the Paschal celebrations of the Easter Triduum. We follow Jesus along the way of his passion and cross, yet always in the yearning toward Easter. To the expression of our Lord's suffering, we join the prayers of intercession for the broken world that his prayer and his life embrace. The prayers need not be printed, except in the case of the opening prayers when they are prayed in unison. Pastoral sensitivity with respect to free prayer needs to be exercised; the need may vary from place to place, and even from one day to the next, depending upon events in the commuity and upon the people gathered. In no case should the prayers neglect the more universal themes and petitions expressed in the texts given. Those intercessions may be used as models.

Worshipers are increasingly receptive to nonverbal witness to the Holy Week events. With such extensive use of readings from the Bible during these days, nonverbal dimensions are not to be overlooked. In some cases, visual arts can create prayerful and meditative environments as well as strong commentary on Scripture. Images of the passion are vivid and varied: the jar of costly perfume, thirty pieces of silver, spears and swords and clubs, the crowing rooster, cross and nails, a crown of thorns, wheat and grapes, a lamb for sacrifice, and others. Projected images or banners, preferably without words, may provide a focus for silent meditation. Liturgical dance or simple mime may enact the events or themes from Scripture. These may be woven together into a unity with silences and prayer, together with appropriate hymnody, choral pieces, or instrumental music. The key to this is thoughtful preparation and a deep simplicity arising out of meditation on the principal texts to be used.

One further dimension of our worship during these final days of Lent deserves special mention, fasting and almsgiving. While the pattern of fasting and almsgiving for Lent cannot be legislated or imposed apart from pastoral realities in local churches, these final days present an especially appropriate time for such practices, so largely missing in contemporary Protestant circles. For example, a partial fast could accompany the midday or evening services Monday through Wednesday. The family setting could include a "sacrificial meal" in which money normally spent for the supper would be contributed by the household or assembled group for a special project such as world hunger or a local need.

Good Friday is, of course, the traditional day of fasting for Christians. In the first three centuries, the Paschal celebrations were always preceded by a two-day fast, and in some cases a modified fast took place over six days. This was mentioned in Athanasius' Festal Letter in A.D. 329. The practices of fasting and almsgiving were taught by Jesus and were widespread in the apostolic church. In contrast to the lenten restraint that recalls our sinfulness, the Easter feast makes evident the abundance of God's goodness which we are empowered to share with others.

In any event, we need to recover the connection between fasting, almsgiving, and prayer. This can be especially meaningful during the prayer vigils on Friday and Saturday of Holy Week. The great Easter celebration, whether the vigil or the first service of Easter Sunday, then breaks the fast after the baptismal initiation of those who, with the whole church, have prepared themselves throughout the lenten season.

VI.

Maundy Thursday: An Order of Worship for Holy Communion with Commentary, Including Provision for Footwashing, an Agapé Meal, or Tenebrae

Introduction

On this night we remember and celebrate the final supper Jesus shared with his disciples in the context of Passover. This event, which reveals the holiness of all subsequent meals eaten in his name, institutes the mystery of his abiding redemptive presence in the church's celebrations of the Lord's Supper, or Eucharist. This evening also marks the beginning of the most solemn and joyful celebration of the entire Christian year. We enter what St. Augustine referred to as "the triduum during which the Lord died, was buried, and rose again."

Historically, Maundy Thursday has included a series of distinctive elements, which have been quite complex and elaborate in certain periods, especially in the Middle Ages. Yet there is a profound simplicity about the essentials, since they arise out of Scripture and the early church's worship, which unfolded the meaning of Christ's redemptive action. From the history of this pattern of elements, we have included six: (1) introductory rites emphasizing penitence, (2) the liturgy of the Word of God, (3) footwashing, (4) Holy Communion (with optional agapé meal or love-feast), (5) the stripping of the church, and (6) Tenebrae, or service of the shadows.

Our worship may be simple or elaborate, depending upon the resources and situation of the local community involved. Options will be noted in the rubrics and in the commentary. The order of service with its texts and actions is designed to focus on the central theological and experiential realities arising from the scriptural events we commemorate and relive this night. In the commentary, numerous suggestions are made concerning the inherent drama and flexibility of the whole liturgy.

GATHERING   *Suitable instrumental or choral music may be offered, or the people may assemble in silence.*

GREETING   *The people stand.*
Return to the Lord, the God of all mercies,
for a feast of love has been prepared for his own.

I will bless the Lord at all times.
His praise shall be continually in my mouth.

O taste and see the goodness of the Lord.

Happy are they who take refuge in God.

O magnify the Lord with me,

And let us exalt God's name together.

HYMN   *See* Book of Hymns, *309, 310, 315, 318, 319, 325, 326, 327, 329, 430.*

PRAYERS OF CONFESSION AND PARDON

My brothers and sisters, Christ shows us his love by becoming a humble servant. Let us draw near to God and confess our sin in the truth of his Spirit.

A brief silence for individual reflection.

A. Merciful God, we have not loved you with all our heart and mind and strength and soul. Lord have mercy.

Lord have mercy.

We have not loved our neighbors as you have taught us. Christ have mercy.

Christ have mercy.

We have not fully received the saving grace of your word and life. Lord, have mercy.

Lord, have mercy.

May the Lord have mercy upon you,
Forgive and heal you by his steadfast love
made known to us by the passion, death, and
resurrection of Jesus Christ our Lord.

Amen. Thanks be to God.

Or, following the silent prayers.

B. **Most merciful God,**
We your church confess
that often our spirit has not been that of Christ.
Where we have failed to love one another as he loves us,
Where we have pledged loyalty to him with our lips
and then betrayed, deserted, or denied him.
Forgive us, we pray, and by your Spirit
make us faithful in every time of trial;
Through Jesus Christ our Lord. Amen.

Who is in a position to condemn? Only Christ.
But Christ suffered and died for us, was raised
from the dead and ascended on high for us,
and continues to intercede for us.
Believe the good news:
In the name of Jesus Christ, you are forgiven!

In the name of Jesus Christ, you are forgiven!
Thanks be to God. Amen.

ACT OF PRAISE

FIRST LECTION
    Exodus 12:1-14   (Year A: 1981, 1984, 1987)
    Exodus 24:3-11   (Year B: 1979, 1982, 1985)
    Jeremiah 31:31-34   (Year C: 1980, 1983, 1986)

PSALM OR ANTHEM   Psalm 116:12-19   (Years
                                       A,B,C)

    Antiphon: **I will lift up the cup of salvation**
                and call upon the name of the Lord.

What shall I render to the Lord
    for all his bounty to me?
I will lift up the cup of salvation
    and call upon the name of the Lord
I will fulfill my vows to the Lord
    in the presence of all his people.
Precious in the sight of the Lord
    is the death of his servants.

Antiphon

O Lord, I am your servant;
    I am your servant and the child of your handmaid;
    you have freed me from my bonds.
I will offer you the sacrifice of thanksgiving
    and call upon the name of the Lord.

I will fulfill my vows to the Lord
   in the presence of all his people,
In the courts of the Lord's house,
   in the midst of you, O Jerusalem.
   Hallelujah!

> Antiphon: **I will lift up the cup of salvation**
> **and call upon the name of the Lord.**

SECOND LECTION
   I Corinthians 11:17-32   (Year A: 1981, 1984, 1987)
   I Corinthians 10:16-21   (Year B: 1979, 1982, 1985)
   Hebrews 10:16-30   (Year C: 1980, 1983, 1986)

HYMN or RESPONSORY   *See* Book of Hymns *63,*
162, 257, 259, and 278.

Glory to you, Word of God, Lord Jesus Christ.

Glory to you, Word of God, Lord Jesus Christ.

A new commandment I give to you:
Love one another as I have loved you.

Glory to you, Word of God, Lord Jesus Christ.

THE GOSPEL
   John 13:1-17, 34   (Year A: 1981, 1984, 1987)
   Mark 14:12-26 *or*   (Year B: 1979, 1982, 1985)
   John 13:1-17, 34
   Luke 22:7-30 *or*   (Year C: 1980, 1983, 1986)
   John 13:1-17, 34

SERMON

RESPONSES TO THE WORD

[FOOTWASHING]   *See commentary.*

PRAYERS OF THE PEOPLE

THE PEACE   *The following responsory may be used.*
The Lord Jesus, after he had supped with his disciples
and washed their feet, said to them, "I have given you an
example, that you should do as I have done."

"Peace I leave with you; my peace I give to you;
Peace which the world cannot give, I give to you."

"Love one another, as I have loved you."
The peace of our Lord Jesus Christ be with you all.

And also with you.

Reconciled by his love, let us offer one another
signs of peace and reconciliation.

OFFERING   *The table is prepared during the singing.*

OFFERTORY HYMN or ANTHEM

THE GREAT THANKSGIVING
The Lord be with you.

And also with you.

Lift up your hearts.

We lift them to the Lord.

Let us give thanks to the Lord our God.

It is right to give him thanks and praise.

Blessed are you, Lord of life, Ruler of all things.
You created the heavens and the earth
and saw that it was good.
From the earth you bring forth bread
and create the fruit of the vine.
You formed us in your own image,
called your people by name and made covenant
to be their God and King,
setting before us the way of life.

Therefore we join your whole family of every time,
in heaven and on earth,
for ever praising you and saying (singing):

Holy, holy, holy Lord, God of power and might.
Heaven and earth are full of your glory.
Hosanna in the highest.
Blessed is he who comes in the name of the Lord.
Hosanna in the highest.

Time and again we turned aside and abused your holy
  gifts;
Yet you gave us the crowning gift in your Son Jesus
  Christ.
Emptying himself, that our joy might be full,
he fed the hungry, healed the sick, freed the prisoners,
ate with the scorned and forgotten, washed his disciples'
  feet,
and gave a holy meal as the pledge of his abiding
  presence.

On the night in which he gave himself up for us,
at table with those who would desert him and deny him,
he took bread, gave you thanks, broke it,
and gave it to his disciples, saying:
"Take, eat, this is my body which is given for you.
Do this in remembrance of me."
When the supper was over,
he took the cup, gave you thanks,
and gave it to his disciples, saying:
"Drink this, all of you;
this is my blood which seals God's promise,
poured out for you and for all, for the forgiveness of sins.
Whenever you drink it, do this in remembrance of me."

We remember and proclaim his death and resurrection,
his ascension and his presence through your Holy Spirit.

Accept our offering of praise and thanksgiving,
in union with your Son's self-offering for us.
Send the power of your Holy Spirit
upon us and upon these gifts of bread and wine,
that we may experience anew the presence of Christ,
be renewed as his body and transformed into his likeness,
as we joyfully await his coming in final victory.

Through him, with him, in him,
In the unity of the Holy Spirit,
all glory and honor is yours, Almighty God,
now and for ever. Amen.

As Christ has taught us, we are bold to pray:

THE LORD'S PRAYER   **Our Father . . .**

THE BREAKING OF BREAD

THE GIVING OF BREAD AND THE CUP
Hymns may be sung.

[PRAYER AFTER COMMUNION]
The Lord is with you.

And also with you.

Let us pray: *A brief silence.*
We thank you, holy God,
   for giving us this meal, shared in the Spirit,
   which sustains us with the food and drink of your life;
Grace our lives that we may at the last come to share
   in the heavenly banquet of your kingdom,
Through Jesus Christ our Lord. **Amen.**

[THE STRIPPING OF THE CHURCH]
See commentary.

HYMN   *Where the Tenebrae (see chapter 7) or the footwashing is to follow, this hymn should be chosen to introduce that service. See* Book of Hymns, *especially 427 and 430-33. When it does not follow, the service concludes with the following dismissal with blessing.*

DISMISSAL WITH BLESSING

Go forth in peace to walk the way of his cross and resurrection.

We are sent in the name of the Lord.

My Jesus Christ, who was put to death for our sins, bless you and keep you.

Amen.

May Jesus Christ who was raised to life for our salvation let light shine upon you.

Amen.

May Jesus Christ be your life and peace, now and for ever.

Amen. Thanks be to God.

Commentary

Since Maundy Thursday evening is, both by the solemnity of its meaning and structure and by custom among United Methodists, one of the most significant worship experiences of the year, careful planning is crucial. Decisions regarding the various elements in the whole liturgy and the degree of simplicity or elaboration should be made well in advance, preferably at the beginning of Lent. In this way preparations for the whole Easter Triduum can become part of the lenten discipline of the congregation, and particularly of the worship planning committee, the musicians, and others who may contribute.

A balance between flexibility and a well-ordered set of texts and actions is found in the preceding pages. Careful study and pastorally sensitive imagination may envision various adaptations for local circumstances. If all six of the basic elements are incorporated—introductory penitential rite, the Word of God, footwashing, Holy Communion (or agapé), the stripping of the church, and Tenebrae—the length of the service will last from one and a half to two hours. It could follow a community meal or, in some circumstances, be incorporated into such a meal. On the occasion of the first night of the three high holy days of the Christian year, such a gathering of the whole community is a powerful witness. Depending upon the space available and the room environment as well as the customs of the people, these services may be either quite intimate and casual or highly structured liturgically. The whole service, for example, may take place in a fellowship hall. In any case, the whole service should be understood as evangelical in the most profound sense: a proclamation, encounter, and participation in the mystery of our redemption through the saving action of God in Christ.

While the first part of the service is penitential in nature, there may be extensions of forgiveness and reconciliation that echo and become visible throughout. For example, during the responses to the Word, acts of reconciliation are quite appropriate. If there are persons who have been intentionally separated from the church for a period of time, either from grave sin or out of personal alienation or animosity, and who wish to publicly renew their commitment to the church, this is a most opportune moment. In earlier church practice, public penitents were received by the bishop on Maundy Thursday evening. This may take the form of a brief personal witness and an act of reconciliation with the laying on of hands. The minister may say: "In the name of Jesus Christ you are forgiven and reconciled to his body, the church. As you have witnessed to your faith and new intention, by the mercy of Christ we receive you as restored members in this family of faith. God bless you this night and grant you peace. Amen." Similar words may be used.

Other responses to the Word might include silent meditation, with or without visual images of the passion. This would be particularly suitable if the Tenebrae is not included (either as part of the liturgy of the Word of God, or as the concluding element in the whole service). A choral presentation may also be appropriate, especially if it involves congregational participation.

Also fitting, and a very powerful symbolic response to the Word, is the *rite of footwashing*. This dramatizes vividly the humility and servanthood of Jesus, both on the night of his betrayal and in his continuing presence in our midst. When entered into prayerfully and openly, without embarrassment, it is a clear witness to our own role in his actions. It is a response to his "new commandment"—that we love one another as he has loved us.

In a large congregation it is advisable to select certain representatives from the people. At the designated time, they will be invited to come forward to a place where chairs, a basin and pitcher of water, and towels have already been placed. These articles may also be brought forward by deacons or ushers. Depending upon the context, the minister may wash only one foot of each person, though the mutual footwashing among minister(s) and lay persons would be more symbolic of servanthood. These actions should be clearly visible, yet not overly dramatic. Love and care for one another must be expressed in these ritual gestures. It is best not to include persons for whom this seems unduly embarrassing.

During the footwashing, the choir may sing appropriate pieces or the congregation may sing hymns or songs (see *Book of Hymns* 430, 432, 220, 270, 309, and 310). The actions may be done as well in silence.

Where the congregation is small, it may be possible for everyone to participate. Among the Church of the Brethren, even in larger congregations, this has always been done by the whole congregation. The movement of persons should not be forced or regimented, but natural, with an air of hospitality and care. It can be suggested that where possible the worshipers come in sandals, and it can be made clear that persons are welcome simply to observe rather than participate. Basins may be scattered among the congregation, and a small group may form around each basin; or persons may come forward to the basins as they feel led to participate. Sponge and towel are provided at each basin. Persons who have had their feet washed wash their neighbor's in turn.

As an alternative to washing the feet, the shoes may be wiped with a cloth. Care must be taken to preserve the quiet and dignity of the rite.

A strikingly beautiful hymn text which may be sung by choir and congregation is *Ubi Caritas* ("Where charity and love are found, there is God"). This may be used at the offertory if it is not used here.

Refrain:	Where charity and love are found, there is God.
Verse 1:	The love of Christ has gathered us together into one.
	Let us rejoice and be glad in him.
	Let us fear and love the living God,

and love each other from the depths
of   our hearts.

Refrain repeated

Verse 2:   Therefore when we are together,
                        let us take heed not to be divided in
                            mind.
                        Let there be an end to bitterness and
                            quarrels,
                        an end to strife,
                        and in our midst be Christ our God.

Refrain repeated

Verse 3:   And, in company with the blessed,
                        may we see your face in glory, Christ
                            our God,
                        pure and unbounded joy for ever
                            and for ever.

Refrain repeated

Another text which may be set to a simple melodic line is:
                        Faith, hope, and love,
                        let these endure among you;
                        and the greatest of these is love . . .

Or, other versions of I Corinthians 13 may be employed.
Another well-known hymn that picks up the theme of John
13:35 is "They'll Know We Are Christian by Our Love."

The prayers of the people may be a traditional form for
intercession, such as was included in the services for
Monday through Wednesday of Holy Week above. The
Prayer for the Whole State of Christ's Church from the
Methodist Hymnal, 830, may also be used. Several
alternate forms are provided in the *Book of Common
Prayer (Proposed)*, pages 383-93. If free prayer is invited, it

is best to give a simple form such as "For *N.*, that she/he may be . . . , let us pray to the Lord," with the congregation responding "Lord, have mercy," or "Hear us in your mercy."

The offering is taken as usual. During this time the table is prepared for the celebration of the Lord's Supper, or the agapé (love-feast) if for some reason the Sacrament cannot be celebrated. If the elements are already in place, the cloth coverings may be removed. It is appropriate to use a chalice and several additional drinking vessels if the congregation is large. A whole loaf of specially prepared unsliced bread should be used whenever possible. The containers of wine and the bread may be brought forward by lay persons in procession to the table with the offerings, or brought from a credence table nearby, and placed on the altar table. The sung doxology is not necessary during the bringing of the gifts and offerings. The hymn, *Ubi Caritas* (given above) is particularly suitable for this evening's offertory. Other hymns are 313 and 315-32. It may not be necessary to sing all the verses.

After the ushers and gift-bearers return, the congregation remains standing for the Great Thanksgiving. Note the particular resonance of the prayer on this evening. The service is made even more powerful when, following the Communion, the so-called stripping of the church occurs.

A highly vivid and dramatic way of showing forth the desolation and abandonment of the long night in Gethsemane is through the stripping of the altar table and removal of all textile hangings and candles. This practice dates from the seventh century, and began for the utilitarian purpose of cleaning and washing the church in preparation for Easter. But the stark, bare church reflected so clearly the fitting tone of the occasion that the stripping became an evocative ceremony in its own right. The ceremony is probably best done in complete silence. Altar-table cloths and frontals (if any), pulpit and lectern hangings, banners, and candlesticks or other altar-table furnishings are simply picked up by designated persons and carried out of the sanctuary quietly. In a matter of minutes, the visual aspect of the room is completely changed, and the church remains bare until Easter Eve, when the process is reversed.

If no one is present who is authorized to administer Holy Communion, an agapé meal, or love feast, may be celebrated instead. At the conclusion of the prayers of the people and the sharing of the peace, the congregation may process to a fellowship hall or to another room where a meal has been prepared. The people may wish to sing a familiar hymn on their way, or a psalm could be chanted or sung by the choir, or between choir and people in responsive style. The entire service may take place in the fellowship hall. If this is the case, the food is brought out following the prayers of the people. The following is a brief model order.

READING   John 15:4-5*a*, 8-9

HYMN or SONG

BLESSING OF THE BREAD
At each table a loaf of bread is placed. Each person takes a piece and holds it while this or a similar blessing is prayed.
> Blessed are you, O Lord our God, King of the universe,
>
>> you bring forth bread from the earth to sustain us.
>
> Blessed is your name for all the life and food we
>
>> share this night; through Jesus Christ our Lord.

Amen.

THE MEAL
During the meal various readings may be given, such as Isaiah 25:6-9, I John 4:7-21, and Colossians 3:12-17.

124

BLESSING OF THE CUP

At each table a pitcher of fresh fruit juice is saved, and poured out to each person at the end of the meal, at which time all stand for the blessing prayer.

Blessed are you, O Lord our God, King of the universe,
> who creates the fruit of the vine;

Blessed is your name for refreshing our lives from the cup of life and salvation; through Jesus Christ our Lord. **Amen.**

HYMNS or SONGS OF PRAISE

Especially suitable are Psalms 103 and 107:1-9, 33-34, and Psalm 136 (omitting verses 17-22) which may be sung or recited.

If the footwashing has not occurred earlier, it may follow the love-feast; or if Tenebrae is to be celebrated, the congregation may move back to the sanctuary. If the whole service takes place in the fellowship hall, hymns may be sung during the clearing of the tables. There should be absolute quiet and no distracting dishes remaining for the Tenebrae.

Note again that a fellowship meal, structured in a similar manner, may *precede* the liturgy of the Word and Sacrament as well. In some cases, this may be the Seder meal, the order for which is given in chapter 12.

VII.

Tenebrae:
An Order of Worship
with Commentary

This may be incorporated into the Maundy Thursday
Communion Service. It is, however, most appropriately
used on the evening of Good Friday, marking the beginning
of a prayer vigil through Saturday.

[GATHERING]

[GREETING

And this is the judgment, that the light has come into the
world, and men loved darkness rather than light.

God is light, in whom there is no darkness at all.

For God sent the Son into the world, not to condemn the
world, but that the world might be saved through him.

**Every one who does evil hates the light,
and does not come to the light.**

Come, let us worship in spirit and in truth.]

HYMN   *See* Book of Hymns *427, 430-33.*

OPENING PRAYER
The Lord be with you.

And also with you.

Let us pray: *A brief silence.*
Most gracious God,
  Look with mercy upon your family gathered here
  for whom our Lord Jesus Christ was betrayed,
  given into sinful hands, and suffered death upon the
    cross;
Strengthen our faith and forgive our betrayals
  as we enter the way of his passion;
Through him who lives and reigns with you and the Holy
    Spirit,
  for ever and ever. **Amen.**

THE PASSION OF OUR LORD
*Twelve candles, along with a central Christ candle, remain
lighted through the first five sections of the reading; then
they are extinguished one by one at the conclusion of each
of the next twelve sections. At the last, the Christ candle is
either extinguished, or it may be removed or hidden, and
then returned for the final reading from Isaiah.[8]*

1

It was two days before the Passover and the feast of
Unleavened Bread. The religious leaders who collaborated
with the Roman occupation were conspiring against Jesus.
They had gathered in the palace of Caiaphas the high
priest. This man had received the high priesthood at the
hand of Valerius Gratus, the former Roman governor, and
now retained the office under Pontius Pilate. They all were
planning to arrest and destroy Jesus quietly so as to avoid a
popular revolt among the Jews.

2

At this time Jesus was lodging at Bethany in the house of
Simon the leper. While he was there, a woman approached
and anointed him from an alabaster jar of pure nard. When
his disciples saw the act, they were outraged. "Why this
waste?" they demanded. "Such costly ointment might have
been sold for a large sum and given to the poor." Jesus
responded, "Why do you bother the woman? The poor are
always with you. Indeed, I tell you that, wherever the
gospel is preached throughout the world, what she has done
will told in her memory."

3

Then one of the twelve named Judas, Son of Simon the
Iscariot, went to the chief priests and asked, "What will you
give me if I deliver Jesus to you for the governor?" When
they heard the offer, they were glad and promised Judas
thirty pieces of silver. From that hour he sought an
opportunity to betray Jesus.

4

At the beginning of the feast, when the passover lamb
was sacrificed, the disciples of Jesus approached him and
asked, "Where do you wish us to prepare the Paschal
meal?" Jesus took two of his disciples and instructed them,
"Go into the city, and you will see there a man carrying a
water jar. He will show you a suitable place." The two did
as Jesus commanded. They entered the city where they
found the man with the water jar, who brought them to a
large upper room.

5

When evening had come, Jesus arrived with the twelve.
While they were eating, he said, "I tell you truly that one of
you is going to betray me." The disciples were stunned with
grief and began to protest one after the other, "Surely not

I!" Jesus replied, "The betrayer is one of you dipping his hand in the dish with me. The Son of man is fulfilling Scripture, but woe to that man through whom the Son of man is betrayed." Then Judas slipped out into the night.

One of the readers extinguishes the first candle.

6

As they were eating, Jesus took bread. After reciting the blessing, he broke it and gave it to his disciples as he said, "Take, eat; this is my body." Then taking the cup with the traditional blessing, he gave it to his disciples as he said, "This is my blood of the covenant which is being shed for many. I tell you in truth that I shall not drink again from the fruit of the vine until that day when I drink it fresh in the kingdom of God." Then, having sung a hymn, they left the city for the Mount of Olives.

7

As they walked, Jesus said to his disciples, "You will all desert me this very night. So it is written in the prophet Zechariah, 'Strike the shepherd, and the sheep will be scattered.' " Then Peter protested, "Though all desert, I will remain by you." Jesus replied, "I tell you truly that in this very night, before the cock crows twice you shall deny me three times." Still Peter maintained, "Even though I must die with you, I will never deny you": and so declared all the disciples.

The extinguishing of the second candle.

8

Jesus halted at an olive grove called Gethsemane. Then going apart with Peter, James, and John, he left them on watch and continued a little farther alone. There he fell on his face in anguished prayer. Soon he returned to the three on watch and found them sleeping. Rousing them, he asked Peter, "Could you not watch with me for just one hour?

Watch and pray that you are not put to the test; for the spirit is willing but the flesh is weak." Again Jesus went apart in troubled prayer; and again he returned to find the disciples sleeping, for their eyes were heavy. A third time Jesus withdrew to pray, and a third time he found the disciples sleeping. Then Jesus said, "Sleep on and finish your rest. Now is the time for the Son of man to be delivered into the hands of sinners. Here comes my betrayer."

The extinguishing of the third candle.

9

Jesus had not finished speaking before Judas, one of his own disciples, arrived with a group of Roman soldiers and other armed men from the Temple. Now the betrayer had arranged with the authorities for a sign and had said, "The man whom I kiss is the one you want." In accord with this arrangement Judas went directly to Jesus and cried out, "Greetings, Master." Then he gave him the kiss. Jesus responded, "Judas, would you betray the Son of man with a kiss?"

Immediately the soldiers laid hands on Jesus and held him fast. Then one of the disciples with Jesus drew his sword and cut off an ear from the slave of the high priest; but Jesus said to him, "Sheathe your sword. All who take up the sword will perish by the sword. Do you not know that I can call upon my Father and that he will respond at once with more than twelve legions of angels?" Then turning to the mob, Jesus continued, "Have you come for me as against a rebel bandit with swords and clubs? Why did you not seize me in the Temple, where I sat teaching by day? Were you so afraid of the Jewish people that you must come for me by stealth? Nevertheless, your actions are fulfilling the words of the prophets." Then all of his disciples forsook him and fled.

The extinguishing of the fourth candle.

10

Those who had seized Jesus brought him to Caiaphas, whom the Romans had made a high priest. Peter followed at a distance as far as the courtyard. There he sat with the attendants and warmed himself by the fire. The high priest had gathered his whole council, and they began to arrange the case against Jesus which they would present to Pontius Pilate the governor. The charge was that Jesus claimed to be King of the Jews; and they brought in many false witnesses, but to no avail. Finally two came forward and testified, "We heard this man say, 'I will tear down this temple made with hands and within three days build another not made with hands.' " The testimony was evidence that Jesus claimed an authority over Temple affairs which traditionally belonged only to the rulers of Israel, and in those days Israel was ruled from Rome. Yet even these witnesses were unable to agree on their testimony.

Finally Caiaphas stood up and examined Jesus directly. "Have you no answer to these charges?" demanded the high priest. Jesus remained silent and answered nothing. Then the high priest put the question of kingship in terms of the royal titles "Anointed" and "Son of God." "Are you the Anointed One, the Son of the Blessed?" he probed. Jesus answered, "I am, and you shall see the Son of man seated on the right hand of power and coming in the clouds of heaven." The high priest turned and said, "What need have we of witnesses? He has condemned himself." They all concurred that Jesus was indeed worthy of death.

Then those holding Jesus began to spit on him. They covered his face and were striking him as they taunted him and said, "O Anointed One, prophesy who it is who is striking you."

The extinguishing of the fifth candle.

11

Now Peter was warming himself in the courtyard when a small slave girl entered. She confronted Peter and said, "You also were with this Jesus the Nazarene." Peter quickly gave a denial. "I do not know what you are talking about," he replied and went outside into the gateway. Meanwhile, the cock crowed. The slave girl followed Peter out and said to the bystanders, "This man is one of them." Again Peter denied knowing Jesus. After a little while the bystanders said directly to Peter, "Surely you are one of them, for you speak with a Galilean accent." Then Peter began to swear with an oath, "I do not know this person of whom you are speaking"; but the cock interrupted him as it crowed for the second time. Immediately Peter remembered how Jesus had said to him, "Before the cock crows twice, you will deny me three times." He went out and wept bitterly.

The extinguishing of the sixth candle.

, 12

When morning arrived, all of the chief priests, along with the other Roman collaborators, bound Jesus and delivered him over to Pontius Pilate, the imperial Roman governor. When Judas saw what was happening, he knew that Jesus was doomed, and he repented. He returned the thirty pieces of silver to the chief priests and confessed, "I have sinned in betraying innocent blood." "What is that to us?" they responded. "That is your affair." Judas threw down the thirty pieces of silver in the Temple. Then he went out and hanged himself. Picking up the silver pieces, the chief priests said, "It is unlawful to put this silver into the treasury; for it is blood money." Whereupon they used the money to buy the Potter's Field for the burial of strangers. Therefore, that field is known to this day as the Field of Blood.

The extinguishing of the seventh candle.

13

Jesus stood before the Roman governor as the accusers made their charge. "We found this man perverting our nation," they said. "He was forbidding us to pay taxes to the Emperor and proclaiming himself Anointed King." The governor asked, "Are you the King of the Jews?" Jesus answered, "You say so." The chief priests were accusing him of many things. Therefore, Pilate again spoke to Jesus. "Have you no answer to give?" he asked. "Look at how many accusations they are making!" Jesus astonished Pilate by remaining silent.

The extinguishing of the eighth candle.

14

At that festival the governor used to release a prisoner, and some were urging Pilate to do so at this time. Now there was a notable rebel in prison with those who had committed murder during the insurrection. His name was Jesus Barabbas. Therefore, the chief priests arranged a demonstration to demand Barabbas. Pilate asked them, "Whom do you want me to release for you, Jesus Barabbas or Jesus the Anointed One?" The demonstrators shouted, "Barabbas!" Pilate responded, "What shall I do then with Jesus the Anointed One?" The crowd shouted, "Crucify him!" Pilate continued, "Are you certain of his guilt?" The crowd took up the chant, "Crucify him! Crucify him!" Again Pilate spoke, "Shall I crucify your king?" "We have no king but Caesar," cried the demonstrators. Then Pilate agreed to release Jesus Barabbas, but Jesus the Anointed One he handed over to his soldiers for scourging and crucifixion.

The extinguishing of the ninth candle.

15

The soldiers led Jesus away within the governor's palace. There they assembled the whole battalion. They clothed

Jesus in royal purple. They set a crown of thorns upon his head and shoved a reed between his fingers for a scepter. They began to mock him by kneeling before him and proclaiming, "Hail King of the Jews." They also spat upon him and smote him on the head with a stick. Then, after mocking him, they took away the purple, returned his own clothes, and brought him out to crucify him.

The extinguishing of the tenth candle.

16

On the road they met an African of Cyrene named Simon coming in from the countryside. Him they compelled to carry the cross. They brought Jesus to a place called Golgotha (which means "skull"). There they crucified him. . . . They offered him wine mingled with myrrh, but he refused it. His garments they divided among themselves, casting lots for them. Over his head they inscribed the charge against him, The King of the Jews. Also there were two insurrectionists crucified with him, one to his right and one to his left. Those who passed by were shaking their heads in derision and saying, "So you would destroy the Temple and rebuild it in three days! Save yourself. Come down from the cross." Likewise the priestly collaborators mocked him as they said to one another, "He saved others; himself he cannot save. Let the Anointed One, the King of Israel, come down from the cross that we may see and believe." Even the two crucified with him reviled him.

The extinguishing of the eleventh candle.

17

Now from midday there was darkness over the whole land until three in the afternoon. At that hour Jesus cried out in a loud voice, "Eli, Eli, lema shevaqtani!" words that mean, "My God, my God, why have you forsaken me?" Some of the bystanders said, "Look, he is calling for Elijah." One of them put a sponge full of vinegar on a stick and laid it to his lips. Others said, "Wait! Let us see whether Elijah will come to take him down." Then Jesus having uttered a loud cry, breathed his last breath.

The extinguishing of the twelfth candle, and the Christ candle. A loud noise is made by use of a cymbal or other means of harsh sound; the last section is read in darkness, after which the Christ candle may be returned or relighted.

18

Suddenly the curtain of the Temple was torn in two from the top to the bottom. The earth shook, and the rocks were split. Even the tombs of the dead were opened. Now, when the centurion on watch and the others who were with him saw all that was taking place, they were filled with awe and said, "This man truly was God's royal Son!"

Silence. Then return of light.

[SONG OF THE SUFFERING SERVANT]
Isaiah 53:4-9 [or 4-6]
This may be spoken by the congregation, or sung by the choir, or done responsively.

> Surely he has borne our griefs
> and carried our sorrows;
> yet we esteemed him striken,
> smitten by God, and afflicted.
> But he was wounded for our transgressions,
> he was bruised for our iniquities;
> upon him was the chastisement that made us whole,
> and with his stripes we are healed.
> All we like sheep have gone astray;
> we have turned every one to his own way;
> and the Lord has laid on him
> the iniquity of us all.
>
> He was oppressed, and he was afflicted,
> yet he opened not his mouth;

like a lamb that is led to the slaughter,
and like a sheep that before its shearers is dumb,
so he opened not his mouth.
By oppression and judgment he was taken away;
and as for his generation, who considered
that he was cut off out of the land of the living,
striken for the transgression of my people?
And they made his grave with the wicked
and with a rich man in his death,
although he had done no violence,
and there was no deceit in his mouth.

*Or, one of the following hymns may be sung: 412, 418,
420, 432, 435, or 436.*

DISMISSAL

May Jesus Christ, who for our sake became obedient
unto death, even death on a cross, keep you and
strengthen you this night and for ever. **Amen.**

*All depart in quietness, except those beginning the prayer
vigil.*

Tenebrae: Alternate Form A

*With this form, seven or fourteen candles are used, and the
Christ candle. Then, following each section, one or two
are extinguished until the eighth reading, at which time the
loud nose is made and the Christ candle is hidden or
removed. At suitable times, hymns that express the scene
just portrayed, or express a response to it, may be sung.
See hymns 434, 436, 412, 418, 420, 435, and 436.*

(Year A:	(Year B:	(Year C:
1981, 1984)	1982, 1985)	1980, 1983)
I. Matthew	Mark 14:26-42	Luke 22:39-46
26:30-46		

First candle(s) extinguished.

II. Matthew   Mark 14:43-50   Luke 22:47-53
     26:47-56

Second candle(s) extinguished.

III. Matthew   Mark 14:51-72   Luke 22:54-62
     26:57-75

Third candle(s) extinguished.

IV. Matthew   Mark 15:1-5   Luke 22:63-71
     27:1-5

Fourth candle(s) extinguished

V. Matthew   Mark 15:6-15   Luke 23:1-12
     27:6-23

Fifth candle(s) extinguished.

VI. Matthew   Mark 15:16-20   Luke 23:13-25
     27:24-31

Sixth candle(s) extinguished

VII. Matthew   Mark 15:21-32   Luke 23:26-38
     27:32-44

Seventh candle(s) extinguished.

VIII. Matthew   Mark 15:33-36   Luke 23:39-46
     27:45-50

Christ candle removed or hidden, and harsh sound.

IX. Matthew   Mark 15:38-39   Luke 23:47-56*a*
     27:51-54

Christ candle returned after a brief silence.

SONG OF THE SUFFERING SERVANT
Isaiah 53:4-9 [or 4-6]

[HYMN]

DISMISSAL WITH BLESSING
Go in peace. May Jesus Christ, who for our sake became obedient unto death, even death on a cross, keep you and strengthen you this night and for ever. **Amen.**

All depart in quietness, except those beginning the prayer vigil.

Tenebrae: Alternate Form B

In communities where the passion narrative is read on Palm/Passion Sunday and Good Friday, it is wise to use this form of the Tenebrae, which centers in the reading of appropriate psalms. It may be done on Thursday, Friday, and Saturday of Holy Week. During the first set of psalms, seven candles are extinguished at suitable intervals; during the second set of three psalms, seven more candles are extinguished. All other candles and lights are extinguished during the Benedictus (Luke 1:68–79) except for one candle which is hidden, usually behind the altar table. The people remain seated during the recital of these psalms and the reading from Lamentations, and the Gloria Patri is, of course, not used.

In the darkened church, people may kneel for the Lord's Prayer (which follows the short responsory), for the final Psalm 51 (which may be recited responsively by the choir), and for the final prayer. The hidden candle is brought out again just before the final prayer. The congregation is dismissed and departs in silence.

Thursday	Friday	Saturday
[GATHERING]	GATHERING	GATHERING
[GREETING]	GREETING	GREETING
PSALMS	PSALMS	PSALMS
69, 70, 71	72, 73, 74	2, 22, 27
A READING	A READING	A READING
Lamentations	Lamentations	Lamentations
1:1-14	2:10-19	3:1-21
PSALMS	PSALMS	PSALMS
75, 76, 77	38, 40, 54	59, 88, 94
THE GOSPEL	THE GOSPEL	THE GOSPEL
John 13	John 16	John 17
BENEDICTUS	BENEDICTUS	BENEDICTUS

Blessed be the Lord, the God of Israel;
he has come to his people and set them free.

He has raised up for us a mighty savior,
born of the house of his servant David.
Through his holy prophets he promised of old
    that he would save us from our enemies,
    from the hands of all who hate us.
He promised to show mercy to our fathers
and to remember his holy covenant.
This was the oath he swore to our father Abraham:
to set us free from the hands of our enemies,
free to worship him without fear,
holy and righteous in his sight
    all the days of our life.

You, my child, shall be called the prophet of the
    Most High,
for you will go before the Lord to prepare his way
to give his people knowledge of salvation
by the forgiveness of their sins.
In the tender compassion of our God
the dawn from on high shall break upon us,
to shine on those who dwell in darkness
    and the shadow of death,
and to guide our feet into the way of peace.
              A brief silence.

Christ, for our sake, became obedient unto death;

Even unto the death of the cross.

THE LORD'S PRAYER

    A brief silence; the Christ candle is returned.

[PSALM 51:1-17   *See pp. 35-36 for text.*]

CLOSING PRAYER
Lord Jesus, One of us betrayed you,
    another denied you,
    and all of us have forsaken you.

Yet you remained faithful to death,
  even death upon a cross.
Strengthen us so we do not turn aside
  but follow you through sunlight and shadow alike.
For the final victory belongs to you, Lord Jesus.
Amen.

DISMISSAL
  Go in peace.
  May Jesus Christ, who for our sake became obedient
  unto death, even death on a cross,
  keep you and strengthen you this night and for ever.
  Amen.

All depart in quietness.

Commentary

  The service of Tenebrae or "shadows," grew out of a combination night prayer and early morning prayer, with an additional focus upon the commemoration of the passion. The latter was usually read by several deacons, and later, in the Middle Ages, was read by monastic choirs. The most striking feature of this service is the gradual extinguishing of the lights and candles in the room and on the altar. The bare altar table and the unvested furnishings emphasize the starkness of the events recalled. The candles represent the apostles and all followers of Christ, and the larger candle represents Christ. The dramatic high point occurs with the complete darkness and the loud noise, or *strepitus,* at the death of Jesus.

  This service may be used in one of three ways: (1) as preparation for a Maundy Thursday rite of repentance and forgiveness; (2) as a concluding service following Holy Communion on Maundy Thursday; (3) or as the evening service on Good Friday, particularly as the beginning of a prayer vigil lasting through Saturday, or in a retreat. Alternate Form B may be used on all three evenings.

Three basic alternates for the meditation on the passion are included. The first is a specially composed liturgical interpretation by John T. Townsend;[8] the second uses the Johannine text of the Gospel appointed for the year. The third is based upon psalms of distress, passages from Lamentations, and John's Gospel. In the first two alternatives, the passion narrative is divided into sections, and candles are extinguished at certain specific times. Hymns or psalms may also be sung in response to these sections. An atmosphere of quiet and sober reflection should permeate the readings and the prayers. Several readers may be used, alternating the sections. The readers also extinguish the candles.

Care should be taken to rehearse the readings for pace, audibility, and coherent meaning. The larger candle is either hidden at the death passage or removed from the room. Such actions must not be hurried. When the candle is removed, after suitable time for silence in total darkness, it is returned; and the lights of the room are at least partially turned up for the final reading and dismissal.

Alternate Form B provides several possibilities for reciting the psalms. Visuals may be appropriate between the psalms for meditation. The Benedictus (Luke 1:68-79) may be recited or sung by the choir, or it may be recited reponsively by the congregation. Because this will be done in diminishing light, provision must be made for seeing the texts. The brief response which follows should be known by the congregation beforehand. The penitential Psalm 51 is optional, and the closing prayer is prayed by the minister or lay leader. Care should be taken to allow space for silence between the readings.

141

VIII.

Good Friday:
An Order of Worship
with Commentary
and Provision
for a Prayer Vigil
Through Holy Saturday

GATHERING   *The altar table is bare, as the textiles and other furnishings have been removed during the Maundy Thursday service. The cross remains, veiled if possible. Appropriate choral or instrumental music may be offered while the people gather, though silence is preferable. The ministers and readers enter in silence. A brief introduction may be given if necessary. After another silence, the minister invites the people to stand; then he says:*

Blessed be the name of the Lord our God.

Who redeems us from sin and death.

For us and for the salvation of all,
Christ became obedient unto death, even death on a
    cross.

Blessed be the name of the Lord.

HYMN   *See especially* Book of Hymns *415-18, 420, 426-30.*

OPENING PRAYER
Let us pray: *A brief pause.*
Holy and everliving God,
   by the suffering and death of Jesus
   you save us from Adam's fall;
Grant in your mercy that we may be drawn
   to Christ lifted high on the cross,
   and by his redeeming love be raised
   to everlasting life with him,
Who lives and reigns with you in the Holy Spirit,
   for ever and ever. **Amen.**

FIRST LECTION   Isaiah 52:13–53:12   (Years A,B,C)

PSALM or ANTHEM   Psalm 22:1-18 (or 1-11, 18)
My God, my God, why have you forsaken me?
   and are so far from my cry
   and from the words of my distress?
O my God, I cry in the daytime, but you do not answer;
   by night as well, but I find no rest.

Yet you are the Holy One,
   enthroned upon the praises of Israel.
Our ancestors put their trust in you;
   they trusted in you and were not put to shame.

But as for me, I am a worm, and no man,
   scorned by all and despised by the people.
All who see me laugh me to scorn;
   they curl their lips and wag their heads, saying,
"He trusted in the Lord; let him deliver him;
   let him rescue him, if he delights in him."

Yet you are the one who took me out of the womb,
   and kept me safe upon my mother's breast.
I have been entrusted to you ever since I was born;
   you were my God when I was still in my mother's
      womb.
Be not far from me, for trouble is near,
   and there is none to help.

Many young bulls encircle me;
   strong bulls of Bashan surround me.
They open wide their jaws at me,
   like a ravening and a roaring lion.

I am poured out like water;
   all my bones are out of joint;
   my heart within my breast is melting wax.
My mouth is dried out like a potsherd;
   my tongue sticks to the roof of my mouth;
   and you have laid me in the dust of the grave.

Packs of dogs close me in,
   and gang of evildoers circle around me;
   they pierce my hands and my feet;
I can count all my bones.
   They stare and gloat over me;
they divide my garments among them;
   they cast lots for my clothing.

SECOND LECTION   Hebrews 4:14-16; 5:7-9 *or*
Hebrews 10:1-25   (Years A,B,C)

HYMN or RESPONSORY
   Christ became obedient unto death,
   even death on a cross.

   Have mercy on us, Lord Jesus.

144

Therefore, God raised him on high
and gave him a name above all other names.

Praise to you, Lord Jesus Christ.

THE PASSION OF OUR LORD ACCORDING TO JOHN
John 18:1–19:42 [or 19:17-30]
This is most suitably proclaimed as a dramatic reading. Specific roles may be assigned. The principal designations are: N–narrator; †–Christ; S–speakers other than Christ (these may be divided into separate male and female voices, indicated by S₁, S₂, S₃, and Sps); C–crowd (or congregation).

N   Jesus . . . went forth with his disciples across the Kidron valley, where there was a garden, which he and his disciples entered. Now Judas, who betrayed him, also knew the place; for Jesus often met there with his disciples. So Judas, procuring a band of soldiers and some officers from the chief priests and the Pharisees, went there with lanterns and torches and weapons. Then Jesus, knowing all that was to befall him, came forward and said to them,

†   "Whom do you seek?"

N   They answered him,

Sps   "Jesus of Nazareth."

N   Jesus said to them,

†   "I am he."

N   Judas, who betrayed him, was standing with them. When he said to them, "I am he," they drew back and fell to the ground. Again he asked them,

† "Whom do you seek?"

N And they said,

Sps "Jesus of Nazareth."

N Jesus answered,

† "I told you that I am he; so, if you seek me, let these men go."

N This was to fulfil the word which he had spoken, "Of those whom thou gavest me I lost not one." Then Simon Peter, having a sword, drew it and struck the high priest's slave and cut off his right ear. The slave's name was Malchus. Jesus said to Peter,

† "Put your sword into its sheath; shall I not drink the cup which the Father has given me?"

N So the band of soldiers and their captain and the officers of the Jews seized Jesus and bound him. First they led him to Annas; for he was the father-in-law of Caiaphas, who was high priest that year. It was Caiaphas who had given counsel to the Jews that it was expedient that one man should die for the people.

Simon Peter followed Jesus, and so did another disciple. As this disciple was known to the high priest, he entered the court of the high priest along with Jesus, while Peter stood outside at the door. So the other disciple, who was known to the high priest, went out and spoke to the maid who kept the door, and brought Peter in. The maid who kept the door said to Peter,

S_1 "Are not you also one of this man's disciples?"

N   He said,

S₂   "I am not."

N   Now the servants and officers had made a charcoal fire, because it was cold, and they were standing and warming themselves; Peter also was with them, standing and warming himself.

       The high priest then questioned Jesus about his disciples and his teaching. Jesus answered him,

†   "I have spoken openly to the world; I have always taught in synagogues and in the temple, where all Jews come together; I have said nothing secretly. Why do you ask me? Ask those who have heard me, what I said to them; they know what I said."

N   When he had said this, one of the officers standing by struck Jesus with his hand, saying,

S₃   "Is that how you answer the high priest?"

N   Jesus answered him,

†   "If I have spoken wrongly bear witness to the wrong; but if I have spoken rightly, why do you strike me?"

N   Annas then sent him bound to Caiaphas the high priest.

       Now Simon Peter was standing and warming himself. They said to him,

Sps   "Are not you also one of his disciples?"

N   He denied it and said,

S₂   "I am not."

N   One of the servants of the high priest, a kinsman of the man whose ear Peter had cut off, asked,

147

S₄   "Did I not see you in the garden with him?"

N   Peter again denied it; and at once the cock crowed.
       Then they led Jesus from the house of Caiaphas to the praetorium. It was early. They themselves did not enter the praetorium, so that they might not be defiled, but might eat the Passover. So Pilate went out to them and said,

S₅   "What accusation do you bring against this man?"

N   They answered him,

Sps   "If this man were not an evildoer, we would not have handed him over."

N   Pilate said to them,

S₅   "Take him yourselves and judge him by your own law."

N   The Jews said to him,

Sps   "It is not lawful for us to put any man to death."

N   This was to fulfil the word which Jesus had spoken to show by what death he was to die.
       Pilate entered the praetorium again and called Jesus, and said to him,

S₅   "Are you the King of the Jews?"

N   Jesus answered,

†   "Do you say this of your own accord or did others say it to you about me?"

N   Pilate answered,

S₅   "Am I a Jew? Your own nation and the chief priests have handed you over to me; what have you done?"

N   Jesus answered,

†   "My kingship is not of this world; if my kingship were of this world, my servants would fight, that I might not be handed over to the Jews; but my kingship is not from the world."

N   Pilate said to him,

S_5 "So you are a king?"

N   Jesus answered,

†   "You say that I am a king. For this I was born, and for this I have come into the world, to bear witness to the truth. Every one who is of the truth hears my voice."

N   Pilate said to him,

S_5 "What is truth?"

N   After he had said this, he went out to the Jews again, and told them,

S_5 "I find no crime in him. But you have a custom that I should release one man for you at the Passover; will you have me release for you the King of the Jews?"

N   They cried out again,

Sps   "Not this man, but Barabbas!"

N   Now Barabbas was a robber.
     Then Pilate took Jesus and scourged him. And the soldiers plaited a crown of thorns, and put it on his head, and arrayed him in a purple robe; they came up to him, saying,

Sps   "Hail, King of the Jews!"

N   and struck him with their hands. Pilate went out again, and said to them,

S₅   "See, I am bringing him out to you, that you may know that I find no crime in him."

N   So Jesus came out, wearing the crown of thorns and the purple robe. Pilate said to them,

S₅   "Behold the man!"

N   When the chief priests and the officers saw him, they cried out,

C   "Crucify him, crucify him!"

N   Pilate said to them,

S₅   "Take him yourselves and crucify him, for I find no crime in him."

N   The Jews answered him,

C   "We have a law, and by that law he ought to die, because he has made himself the Son of God."

N   When Pilate heard these words, he was the more afraid; he entered the praetorium again and said to Jesus,

S₅   "Where are you from?"

N   But Jesus gave no answer. Pilate therefore said to him,

S₅   "You will not speak to me? Do you not know that I have power to release you, and power to crucify you?"

N   Jesus answered him,

†   "You would have no power over me unless it had been given you from above; therefore he who delivered me to you has the greater sin."

N   Upon this Pilate sought to release him, but the Jews cried out,

Sps   "If you release this man, you are not Caesar's friend; every one who makes himself a king sets himself against Caesar."

N   When Pilate heard these words, he brought Jesus out and sat down on the judgment seat at a place called The Pavement, and in Hebrew, Gabbatha. Now it was the day of Preparation for the Passover; it was about the sixth hour. He said to the Jews,

S₅   "Behold your King!"

N   They cried out,

C   "Away with him, away with him, crucify him!"

N   Pilate said to them,

S₅   "Shall I crucify your King?"

N   The chief priests answered,

Sps   "We have no king but Caesar."

N   Then he handed him over to them to be crucifed.

(Short form.)

[So they took Jesus, and he went out, bearing his own cross, to the place called the place of a skull, which is called in Hebrew Golgotha. There they crucified him, and with him two others, one on either side, and Jesus between them. Pilate also wrote a title and put it on the cross; it read, "Jesus of Nazareth, the King of the Jews." Many of the Jews read this title, for the place where Jesus was crucified was near the city; and it was written in Hebrew, in Latin, and in Greek. The chief priests of the Jews then said to Pilate,

Sps   "Do not write, 'The King of the Jews,' but, 'This man said, I am King of the Jews.' "

N   Pilate answered,

S₅   "What I have written I have written."

N   When the soldiers had crucified Jesus they took his garments and made four parts, one for each soldier. But his tunic was without seam, woven from top to bottom; so they said to one another,

Sps   "Let us not tear it, but cast lots for it to see whose it shall be."

N   This was to fulfil the scripture. "They parted my garments among them, and for my clothing they cast lots."

So the soldiers did this. But standing by the cross of Jesus were his mother, and his mother's sister, Mary the wife of Clopas, and Mary Magdalene. When Jesus saw his mother, and the disciple whom he loved standing near, he said to his mother,

†   "Woman, behold your son!"

N   Then he said to the disciple,

†   "Behold your mother!"

N   And from that hour the disciple took her to his own home.

After this Jesus, knowing that all was now finished, said (to fulfil the scripture),

†   "I thirst."

N   A bowl full of vinegar stood there; so they put a sponge full of the vinegar on hyssop and held it to his mouth. When Jesus had received the vinegar, he said,

†   "It is finished";

N   and he bowed his head and gave up his spirit.]

(Short form ends.)

Since it was the day of Preparation, in order to prevent the bodies from remaining on the cross on the sabbath (for that sabbath was a high day), the Jews asked Pilate that their legs might be broken, and that they might be taken away. So the soldiers came and broke the legs of the first, and of the other who had been crucified with him; but when they came to Jesus and saw that he was already dead, they did not break his legs. But one of the soldiers pierced his side with a spear, and at once there came out blood and water. He who saw it has borne witness—his testimony is true, and he knows that he tells the truth—that you also may believe. For these things took place that the scripture might be fulfilled. "Not a bone of him shall be broken." And again another scripture says, "They shall look on him whom they have pierced."

After this Joseph of Arimathea, who was a disciple of Jesus, but secretly, for fear of the Jews, asked Pilate that he might take away the body of Jesus, and Pilate gave him leave. So he came and took away his body. Nicodemus also, who had at first come to him by night, came bringing a mixture of myrrh and aloes, about a hundred pounds' weight. They took the body of Jesus, and bound it in linen cloths with the spices, as is the burial custom of the Jews. Now in the place where he was crucified there was a garden, and in the garden a new tomb where no one had ever been laid. So because of the Jewish day of Preparation, as the tomb was close at hand, they laid Jesus there.

[SERMON]

HYMN

PRAYERS OF THE PEOPLE
The minister or other appointed person may say:

My brothers and sisters: God sent Christ into the world, not to condemn the world, but that the world through him might be saved; that all who believe in him might be delivered from the power of sin and death, and become heirs with him of everlasting life.

Therefore, let us pray with the whole church for people everywhere in their needs, and for the whole world.

See pages 98-99, 122-23 and the commentary.
The service concludes with one of the following alternates.

Alternate A: A Brief Closing
HYMN or ANTHEM

LORD'S PRAYER

[CONCLUDING PRAYER
Lord Jesus Christ, Son of God,
    set your passion, cross, and death between your
    judgment and our souls, now and in the hour of our
        death.

154

Give mercy and grace to the living;
pardon and rest to the dead and the dying;
to your church, peace and unity;
and to us sinners, everlasting life;
For you live and reign with the Father and the Holy
Spirit,
one God, now and for ever. **Amen.**]

All depart in silence.

Alternate B: Meditations on the Cross
Following the prayers, a wooden cross may be brought silently into the church and positioned in a visible and accessible place. If there is a procession, the following verse and response may be said or sung two or three times by the ministers, the choir, and the people—pausing at the place in the church where it is sung—depending upon the space involved.

This is the wood of the cross, on which hung
the Savior of the world.
Come let us worship and bow down.

After the cross has been positioned, a hymn or choral and congregational setting of the following hymns or anthems may be said or sung.

HYMN or RESPONSIVE ANTHEM
See Book of Hymns *426, 430, 432, 435, 436, 418, 420,* and *228.*

and/or

We glory in your cross, O Lord,

and praise and glorify your resurrection victory;
for by virtue of your cross
joy has come to the whole world.

May God be merciful to us and bless us,
shed the light of his countenance on us, and come to us.

**We glory in your cross, O Lord,
and praise and glorify your resurrection,
for by virtue of your cross
joy has come to the whole world.**

or

**We adore you, O Christ, and we bless you,
By your holy cross you have redeemed the world.**

If we have died with him, we shall also live with him;
if we endure, we shall also reign with him.

**We adore you, O Christ, and we bless you,
By your holy cross you have redeemed the world.**

or

O Savior of the world,
who by your cross and precious blood did redeem us:
Help, save, pity, and defend us, we pray, O Lord.

SILENT MEDITATION or
DEVOTIONS AT THE CROSS

*In some circumstances, the ministers and the congregation
may wish to come forward in an informal procession to
the cross, with each person making a sign of reverence
such as touching the cross, kneeling briefly, or bowing.
The people should move freely, and return to their seats.
No one should be coerced or regimented.*

*During this time any or all of the following Re-
proaches—questions and responses of Christ's lament
against his faithless church—may be sung or spoken, with
the congregation responding.*

1. Is it nothing to you, all you who pass by?
   Look and see if there is any sorrow like my sorrow
   which was brought upon me,

which the Lord inflicted on the day of his fierce
anger.

Holy God,
Holy and Mighty.
Holy and Immortal One,
Have mercy upon us.

2. O my people, O my church,
What have I done to you,
or in what have I offended you?
Testify against me.
I led you forth from the land of Egypt
and delivered you by the waters of baptism,
but you have prepared a cross for your Savior.

Holy God,
Holy and Mighty.
Holy and Immortal One,
Have mercy upon us.

3. I led you through the desert forty years,
and fed you with manna:
I brought you through tribulation and penitence,
and gave you my body, the bread of heaven,
but you have prepared a cross for your Savior.

Holy God . . .

4. What more could I have done for you
that I have not done?
I planted you, my chosen and fairest vineyard,
I made you the branches of my vine;
but when I was thirsty, you gave me vinegar to drink,
and pierced with a spear the side of your Savior.

Holy God . . .

5. I went before you in a pillar of cloud,
and you have led me to the judgment hall of Pilate.

I scourged your enemies and brought you to a land of
  freedom,
but you have scourged, mocked, and beaten me.
I gave you the water of salvation from the rock,
but you have given me gall and left me to thirst.

Holy God . . .

6. I gave you a royal scepter,
   and bestowed the keys to the kingdom,
   but you have given me a crown of thorns.
   I raised you on high with great power,
   but you have hanged me on the cross.

Holy God . . .

7. My peace I gave, which the world cannot give,
   and washed your feet as a sign of my love,
   but you draw the sword to strike in my name
   and seek high places in my kingdom.
   I offered you my body and blood,
   but you scatter and deny and abandon me.

Holy God . . .

8. I sent the Spirit of truth to guide you,
   and you close your hearts to the Counselor.
   I pray that all may be one in the Father and me,
   but you continue to quarrel and divide.
   I call you to go and bring forth fruit.
   but you cast lots for my clothing.

Holy God . . .

9. I grafted you into the tree of my chosen Israel,
   and you turned on them with persecution and mass
     murder.
   I made you joint heirs with them of my covenants,
   but you made them scapegoats for your own guilt.

Holy God . . .

10. I came to you as the least of your brothers and
   sisters;
   I was hungry and you gave me no food,
   I was thirsty and you gave me no drink,
   I was a stranger and you did not welcome me,
   naked and you did not clothe me,
   sick and in prison and you did not visit me.

Holy God . . .
   A brief silence follows.

LORD'S PRAYER

[CONCLUDING PRAYER]
   All depart in silence.

Commentary

Many local churches have an already established
tradition of a two or three hour service on Good Friday
afternoon, usually beginning at noon. It is often ecumenical
in nature. In many places the service is based upon the
Word of God and upon musical offerings, focusing on the
seven last words of Christ, a composite of several Gospel
accounts, with hymns and music by a number of composers.

The service presented here is designed to focus even
more intensely on the proclamatory reading and experience of the context and meaning of the crucifixion for us
today. In particular, it uses the passion according to Saint
John, since the three Synoptic Gospels are used on
Palm/Passion Sunday. This service has three principal
sections: the proclamation of the Word of God, the
intercessory prayers for the afflictions of the world, and the
meditations at the cross. The latter section may be omitted,
or other suitable devotions may be substituted, such as the

"stations" of the cross or silent prayer with directed reflection or hymns and free prayer. The service can easily incorporate parts of various musical settings of the Saint John Passion, of which the most well-known is that of J. S. Bach.

As with other services for Holy Week and Easter Triduum, this may be quite simple in style and relatively brief; or it may be more elaborate and fully developed, depending upon the resources and the local circumstances. The more elaborated devotional form could last up to two hours.

A sizable wooden cross (for example, six feet by four feet) may be positioned before the service in the narthex or foyer of the building, or just outside the main entrance. Then, following the prayers of the people, it may be brought in procession as indicated. Several persons may take part in the procession, including lay persons. In this manner the congregation passes by the wooden cross upon entering, and then again experiences the cross as a focus for meditation and devotional acts as the concluding section of the service.

Many United Methodists have found that nonverbal expressions of devotion to Christ and the cross are powerful though somewhat unfamiliar. It is crucial that the sign-acts with the cross be introduced in prayerful reflection and discussion with the work area on worship or the worship committee well before the Good Friday service. If possible, the congregation may be instructed as well. More harm than good may result without careful teaching and pastoral direction here. On the other hand, Alternate B should be considered by each congregation since it provides a strong expression of encounter and witness to the redeeming love of Christ, echoing the Wesleys' devotion to the wounds of Christ.

With respect to the service of the Word, the reading of

the passion may be shortened, if necessary, to John 19:17-30 (indicated by brackets in the text). In some cases, chancel drama may be used and integrated into the whole of the service. Hymns may be interspersed at appropriate intervals within the reading, as was suggested for Palm/Passion Sunday and the service of Tenebrae.

A special word must be said concerning the Reproaches. Traditionally these were used to dramatize the accusations that God brings against his people in light of the passion and death of Christ. They ask questions that reveal our own rebellion and complicity in the sufferings of Christ and in the evil and sufferings in the world. Images from Scripture are used concerning Israel and God's hand in that holy history, but the accusations are clearly aimed at the faithlessness of all who would call upon God, particularly at all Chrstians in the church who presume to be grafted into the tree of Israel (Romans 11:17-24). The accusations are like an inversion of the holy history we recite and recall in the Great Thanksgivings at the Lord's table.

We must all be aware however, of the history of anti-Jewish sentiment which has often seen the crucifixion to be the work of the Jews. This is abhorrent, especially in light of modern consequences of anti-Semitism, and its continuing presence within the Christian community. For those situations where the Reproaches may give the impression of anti-Jewish convictions, they should not be used. But these texts have been carefully recast, based upon the excellent work done by the Inter-Lutheran Commission on Worship and upon serious reflection. In fact, by the inclusion of verse 9, the Reproaches become a specific act of repentance by Christians for anti-Semitism, appropriate to the day that has been the occasion in our history for overt expressions of anti-Semitism.

If all ten verses are too many for a given service, only those verses which are most appropriate may be used.

Verses 1, 2, 6, 7, and 8 are one possible shortened form. It is also possible to create a contemporary version from images born of our own rebellion and abuse of God's good gifts—though care should be taken not to make this ecological alone; the *theological* point of the accusations and responses is central. This may be done visually using slides or other projections of events, persons, and situations which show us our complicity in rejecting Christ. The images from verse 10 are particularly suggestive and are based upon Matthew 25.

When Tenebrae is not celebrated on Maundy Thursday, it is quite appropriate for Good Friday evening. Increasing numbers of churches are holding continuous prayer vigils from Friday evening through the afternoon on Holy Saturday. One possibility is to use the Tenebrae service described in chapter 7 as the beginning of such a prayer vigil. Persons and families sign up for certain designated hours (in thirty- or sixty-minute periods). The church building would be open during these hours up to the beginning of the Easter Vigil on Saturday evening. A set of resources might be provided, based upon the images and the passion narrative, to those who keep vigil. This could take the form of a brief printed set of meditations and prayers or a tape of directed meditation or a tableau of images or icons. The persons would bring their own Bibles.

Holy Saturday

On Holy Saturday, the church continues in prayer, waiting with the women at the Lord's tomb. The meditation continues to focus upon the themes of redemptive suffering and death. The altar table remains bare. If a brief liturgy of the Word is part of the devotions of those on the prayer vigil—say at noon—it could be patterned after the

Alternate Form B of Tenebrae. Or the following may be used.

PRAYER

Merciful and ever-living God,
creator of heaven and earth:
As the crucified body of your Son was laid in the tomb
and rested on this holy day,
Grant that we may await with him the dawning
of the third day as he promised,
and rise with him in newness of life;
Through Jesus Christ our Lord. **Amen.**

READINGS

Job 14:1-14
Psalm 130 or Psalm 31:1-5 as responsorial psalms
I Peter 4:1-8
Matthew 27:57-66 or John 19:38-42

RESPONSORY

In the midst of life we are in death;
from whom can we seek help?
From you alone, O Lord,
who by our sins are justly angered.

Holy God, Holy and Mighty,
Holy and merciful Savior,
Deliver us from the bitterness of eternal death.

Good Friday and Holy Saturday are traditional days of fasting. The whole church may be invited to fast along with those on prayer vigil or on retreat during this period.

These two days are also a significant time for a retreat. Historically, these hours were the last period of intensive preparation for those persons who were to be baptized at the first Easter service—in ancient times, always the great

Easter Vigil. We wish to encourage this possibility. Such a retreat may be for any group within the church. Elements of the Good Friday services, both the afternoon sections and the Tenebrae, may be used to structure common prayer. There should be periods of common prayer and reflection on Scripture, with times for personal solitude throughout the day. In the case of those preparing for Baptism, some of the great patristic (early church) writings, catechetical lectures, and Easter homilies may be read and shared. Writings of Saint Ambrose, Saint John Chrysostom, Saint Cyril of Jerusalem, and Theodor of Mopsuestia are rich in instruction and spiritual insight for this period. These may be found in Edward Yarnold's *The Awe-Inspiring Rites of Initiation: Baptismal Homilies of the Fourth Century* (London: St. Paul's Publications, 1971).

IX.

Easter Vigil
or The First Service
of Easter:
An Order of Worship
with Commentary

Introduction
(The following introductory remarks may be duplicated and distributed to the congregation as part of their preparation for Holy Week. In churches celebrating the vigil for the first time, a preparatory meeting or study group may be formed during Lent.)

During the Easter Triduum, from sunset Thursday to sunset Sunday, we celebrate the saving events of our Lord's passion, death, and resurrection. In the development of Christian worship, each event came to be remembered on a separate day. In the earliest centuries, however, the whole of the Paschal Mystery was celebrated in an extraordinary single liturgy which began on Saturday night and continued until the dawn of what we now call Easter Sunday. This was known as the great Paschal (Easter) Vigil. It was the most holy and joyful night of the entire Christian year, for it proclaimed and celebrated the whole of salvation history and Christ's saving work.

On this holy and joyous Paschal night, the fullness of the sacraments of Christian initiation are joined to the Word of God, as we participate in the passing from death to life, and to rebirth into the kingdom of God. Justin Martyr, writing in the second century, tells us that persons preparing for Baptism fasted as discipline. By the fourth century the period of preparation and instruction lasted forty days (the origin of our modern Lent). In his *Homilies,* Saint Basil declares: "What time is more appropriate for Baptism than this day of the Pasch? It is the memorial day of the resurrection. Baptism implants in us the seed of resurrection. Let us then receive the grace of resurrection on the day of the resurrection."[9] The whole community's participation in this most dramatic occasion of worship reveals the original unity of the rites of Christian initiation. This liturgy is for all members of the household of faith and presents the grace of renewal which is at the heart of being raised to new life in Christ.

The Paschal or Easter Vigil has both historic and symbolic roots in the Jewish Passover. This is why so many images are from the Old Testament and why so many analogies are experienced in Christ. In this service we experience the passage from slavery to freedom, from sin to salvation, from death to life. The vigil of the Christian Passover marks the beginning of the Sunday of all Sundays, the Lord's Day above all others.

In recent times, there has been widespread interest in the recovery of this ancient First Service of Easter. Many United Methodists are familiar with Easter sunrise services and the main Easter morning service bathed in a sea of lilies and special music. Relatively few have celebrated this most glorious and fitting occasion for the Lord's Supper; and fewer still have experienced the intensity of the whole drama of salvation which the Easter Vigil proclaims and presents.

The order of service which follows is patterned after the ancient vigil service. It may be celebrated beginning Saturday night and culminating early Sunday morning after midnight, or as a predawn Sunday morning service. In the former case, we call it the Easter Vigil; in the latter the First Service of Easter. When it is held in the early morning hours, it may be followed by a festive Easter breakfast. In either case, the whole liturgy has four principal parts:

1. The Service of Light
2. The Service of the Word of God
3. The Service of the Water
4. The Service of the Bread and Cup

Two primary characteristics of this celebration are to be noted: first, the dominant symbols of light, water, and the heavenly banquet; and second, the powerful sweep of the Scriptures, the whole history of God's creating and redeeming work focused in Jesus Christ. Thus, we may say that this is at one and the same time the most evangelical, biblical, sacramental, and liturgical occasion of worship in the whole of Christian life.

As with other services in this book, the basic pattern may be carried out quite simply, or in a richly elaborated manner. The pattern and the texts with actions are designed for flexible adaptation without sacrificing the theological depth and meaning of this most glorious gathering in the church's year. The following pattern and texts resemble closely the traditional vigil, which is now being recovered by almost all Christian traditions, and yet allow for distinctively United Methodist accents as well. It may be modified according to pastoral realities and local circumstances; but the integrity of the four principal elements and the primary characteristics should be preserved—especially the sacraments of Baptism (or baptismal renewal) and the Lord's Supper, or Eucharist. If the whole liturgy is celebrated, the people should be made aware of the length of the service, and should prepare accordingly.

1. The Service of Light

The vigil begins in darkness. Wherever possible, the lighting of the new fire should take place outside the building in a suitable place, or in another room or fellowship hall which can accommodate the whole gathering. This allows a congregational procession into the room of worship.

The fire is kindled while some of the people may still be gathering. Silence is kept for a time until all are assembled. Then the presiding minister, or someone appointed, addresses the people with these or similar words:

GREETING AND INTRODUCTION

Grace and peace to you from Jesus Christ our Lord.

My brothers and sisters in Christ: On this most holy night (morning) in which Jesus Christ passed over from death to life, we gather as the church to pray and to watch for the dawning of his triumph and resurrection. We join with the whole company of God's people in heaven and on earth in recalling and celebrating his victory over death, and our deliverance from the bondage of sin and darkness to everlasting light. *A brief pause.*

Hear the Word of God: "In the beginning was the Word, and the Word was with God, and the Word was God. . . . In him was life, and the life was the light of all people. The light shines in the darkness, and the darkness has not overcome it." (John 1:1, 4-5)

OPENING PRAYER

Let us pray: *A brief pause.*

Eternal Lord of life,

Through your Son you have bestowed the light of life upon all the world: Santify this new fire and grant that our hearts and minds also be kindled with holy desire

168

to shine forth with the brightness of Christ's rising, and
to feast at the heavenly banquet;
Through Jesus Christ our Lord. **Amen.**

LIGHTING OF THE PASCHAL CANDLE
The Paschal candle is lighted from the fire, and these words are spoken:

The light of Christ rises in glory,
overcoming the darkness of sin and death.

The candle is lifted that all may see it, and immediately a procession forms, with choir or singers leading the candle-bearers and the ministers, followed by the people, into the sanctuary or worship area.

PROCESSION INTO THE CHURCH
Depending upon the distance, the procession pauses three times at various places—the third being when all are in position in the sanctuary—to sing:

Or a hymn may be sung as the procession enters the church, particularly "Christ, Whose Glory Fills the Skies." If candles have been given to members of the congregation, they may be lighted from others which have been lit from the Paschal candle. As the room fills, other lights and stationary candles may be lit.

EASTER PROCLAMATION

*When the Paschal candle is placed on a stand visible to the
people, the Exsultet is sung or recited. Various forms of this
ancient and glorious hymn are given in the commentary.*

Rejoice, heavenly powers! Sing, choirs of angels!
Exult, all creation around God's throne!
Jesus Christ, our King is risen!
Sound the trumpet of salvation!

Rejoice, O earth, in shining splendor,
   radiant in the brightness of your King!
Christ has conquered! Glory fills you!
Darkness vanishes for ever!

Rejoice, O Holy Church! Exult in glory!
The risen Savior shines upon you!
Let this place resound with joy,
   echoing the mighty song of all God's people!

[My dearest friends, standing with me in this holy light,
   join me in asking God for mercy,
   that he may give his unworthy minister
   grace to sing his Easter praises.
The Lord be with you.

And also with you.]

Lift up your hearts.

We lift them up to the Lord.

Let us give thanks to the Lord our God.

It is right to give him thanks and praise.

It is truly right that with full hearts and
   minds and voices we should praise you,
   invisible, almighty, and eternal God,
   and your only Son, our Lord Jesus Christ.

For Christ has ransomed us with his blood,
   and paid for us the debt of Adam's sin
   to deliver your faithful people.

This is our Passover feast,
   when Christ, the true Lamb, is slain,
   whose blood consecrates the homes of all believers.
This is the night when first you saved our forebearers:
   you freed the people of Israel from their slavery
   and led them dry-shod through the sea.

This is the night when the pillar of fire
   destroyed the darkness of sin!
This is the night when Christians everywhere,
   washed clean of sin and freed from all defilement,
   are restored to grace and grow together in holiness.
This is the night when Jesus Christ broke the chains of
   death and rose triumphant from the grave.

Father, how wonderful you care for us!
How boundless your merciful love!
To ransom a slave you gave away your Son.

[O happy fault, O necessary sin of Adam,
   which gained for us so great a Redeemer!
Most blessed of all nights, chosen by God
   to see Christ rising from the dead!
Of this night scripture says:
   "The night will be as clear as day:
   it will become my light, my joy."

The power of this holy night
   dispels all evil, washes guilt away,
   restores lost innocence, brings mourners joy;
   it casts out hatred, brings us peace,
   and humbles earthly pride.]

Night truly blessed, when heaven is wedded to earth,
and man is reconciled with God!
Therefore, heavenly Father, in the joy of this night,
receive our evening sacrifice of praise,
your church's solemn offering.
Accept this Easter candle,
a flame divided but undimmed,
a pillar of fire that glows to the honor of God.
Let it mingle with the lights of heaven
and continue bravely burning to dispel the darkness of
the night!

May the Morning Star which never sets find this flame
still burning: Christ, that Morning Star, who
came back from the dead,
and shed his peaceful light on all creation,
your Son who lives and reigns for ever and
ever. **Amen.**

[HYMN   *See* Book of Hymns *437, 439, 443, and 450.*]

2. The Service of the Word
The celebrant may say:

Dear sisters and brothers in Christ, we now begin our
solemn vigil. Let us attend to the Word of God, recalling
God's saving deeds in history; and, in the fullness of time,
how God's own Son was sent to be our Redeemer. May the
Holy Spirit illumine our hearts and minds in the hearing of
this Word.

OLD TESTAMENT READINGS
*The number of readings may vary according to the length
of the service, but there should always be at least three from
the Old Testament, including Exodus 14. Each reading is
followed by brief silence or a responsorial psalm, then a
prayer. See the commentary for other variations.*

The Creation   Genesis 1:1–2:3
        Psalm 33:1-11 or "Morning Has Broken"
Let us pray:
Almighty God, who wonderfully created, yet more
    wonderfully restored, the dignity of human nature:
    Grant that we may share the divine life of him who
    humbled himself to share our humanity, through Jesus
    Christ our Lord. **Amen.**

Abraham's obedience   Genesis 22:1-18
                Psalm 33:12-22

Let us pray:
Gracious God of all believers,
    through Abraham's obedience you made known your
    faithful love to countless numbers; by the grace of
    Christ's sacrifice fulfill in your church and in all
    creation the joy of your promise and new cove-
    nant. **Amen.**

Israel's deliverance at the Red Sea
                Exodus 14:15–15:1
        (song)   Exodus 15:1-6, 17-18 or hymn 446 or 448
Let us pray:
God our Savior,
    as once you delivered by the power of your mighty arm
    your chosen Israel through the waters of the sea, so
    now deliver your church and all the peoples of the
    earth from bondage and oppression to rejoice and
    serve you in freedom, through Jesus Christ our
    Lord. **Amen.**

Love calls us back   Isaiah 54:5-14
                Psalm 30:2-6, 11-12

Let us pray:
Holy One of Israel, our Redeemer,
    your love is unending and your covenant is not shaken,
    even when our sin carries us away from you;

173

Take pity again, establish us in righteousness,
and through our Baptism lead us to safety in
Jesus Christ our Lord.   **Amen.**

Salvation offered freely to all   Isaiah 55:1-11
                                        (song)   Isaiah 12:2-6

Let us pray:
Creator of all things,
   you freely offer water to the thirsty and food to the
   hungry; Refresh us by the water of Baptism and feed
   us with the bread and wine of your table, that your
   Word may bear fruit in our lives, and bring all to your
   glorious kingdom; Through Jesus Christ our
   Lord.   **Amen.**

A new heart and a new spirit   Ezekiel 36:16-28
                                        Psalm 42:1-7; 43:3-4

Let us pray:
God of holiness and light,
   in the mystery of dying and rising with Christ
   you have established a new covenant of reconciliation:
   Cleanse our hearts and give a new spirit to all your
   people, that your saving grace may be professed and
   made known to the whole world;
   Through Jesus Christ our Lord.   **Amen.**

The gathering of God's people
                     Zephaniah 3:14-17, 19-20
                     Psalm 98 or hymn 392

Let us pray:
Everliving God of power and light,
   look with mercy on your whole church;
   Bring to completion your lasting salvation,
   that the whole world may see the fallen lifted up,
   the old made new, and all things brought to perfection
   in him through whom all things were made,
   our Lord Jesus Christ.   **Amen.**

174

[GLORY TO GOD IN THE HIGHEST or other suitable act of praise]

NEW TESTAMENT READINGS
Epistle   Romans 6:3-11
Psalm or hymn   Psalm 114
Hallelujah!
When Israel came out of Egypt,
    the house of Jacob from a people of strange
        speech,
Judah became God's sanctuary,
    and Israel his dominion.

The sea beheld it and fled;
    Jordan turned and went back.
The mountains skipped like rams,
    and the little hills like young sheep.

What ailed you, O sea, that you fled?
    O Jordan, that you turned back?
You mountains, that you skipped like rams?
    you little hills like young sheep?

Tremble, O earth, at the presence of the Lord,
    at the presence of the God of Jacob,
Who turned the hard rock into a pool of water
    and flint-stone into a flowing spring.

Gospel   Matthew 28:1-10 (Year A: 1981, 1984, 1987)
         Mark 16:1-8   (Year B: 1979, 1982, 1985)
         Luke 24:1-12   (Year C: 1980, 1983, 1986)

SERMON
A short sermon may be given after any of the Old Testament lections as well, depending upon the length of the service. In any case, the sermon after the Gospel should not be long, since the readings are the proclamation on this night.

3. The Service of the Water
(Baptism and Renewal)

Dear friends in Christ, through the sacrament of Baptism we are initiated into Christ's holy church. God incorporates us into his mighty acts of salvation, giving us a new birth by water and the Spirit. All of this is God's gift to us, offered without price. Through Confirmation and other renewals of the baptismal covenant, we acknowledge what God is doing and affirm our commitment to Christ's church.

If a litany of the saints if used, the following may be said:

In this we enter the communion of saints, the church throughout all ages, in heaven and on earth. Let us pray with them and in their strength and company. Surrounded by so great a cloud of witnesses, let us pray to the ever-living God:

[LITANY OF THE SAINTS]   *See commentary.*

PRAYERS FOR THE CHURCH
Special prayers for the universal church and its faith and mission are made, ending with a prayer for those about to be baptized, or about to renew their baptismal promises. The congregation responds to each:
Lord of all ages, hear our prayer.

PRESENTATION OF CANDIDATES *(if any)*
I present *(name[s])*, seeking admission into the Body of Christ through Baptism.
and/or
I present *(name[s])*, for confirmation.

DECLARATION OF REPENTANCE AND
COMMITMENT   *(All the people respond.)*
Do you reject the bondage of sin and accept the liberty which God gives you [and do you pledge to encourage these whom you sponsor to do the same]?

I do.

Do you confess Jesus Christ as your Lord and Savior and pledge allegiance to the kingdom which he has opened to all people of all ages, nations, and races?

I do.

Will you resist evil, injustice, and oppression in whatever guises they present themselves and assist *these* whom you sponsor to recognize and resist them?

I do.

As members of Christ's holy church, you are invited to join now with these persons in receiving and professing the Christian faith as contained in the Scriptures of the Old and New Testaments.

Do you believe in God the Father?

I believe in God, the Father almighty,
   creator of heaven and earth.

Do you believe in Jesus Christ?

I believe in Jesus Christ, his only Son, our Lord.
[He was conceived by the power of the Holy Spirit
   and born of the Virgin Mary.
He suffered under Pontius Pilate,
   was crucified, died, and was buried.
He descended to the dead.
On the third day he rose again.
He ascended into heaven,
   and is seated at the right hand of the Father.
He will come again to judge the living and the dead.]

Do you believe in the Holy Spirit?

I believe in the Holy Spirit,
   [the holy catholic church,
   the communion of saints,

177

the forgiveness of sins,
the resurrection of the body,
and the life everlasting.]

THANKSGIVING OVER THE WATER
The Lord be with you.

And also with you.

Let us pray: *A brief pause.*
Eternal God:
When nothing existed but chaos,
  you swept across the dark waters and brought forth
    light.
In the days of Noah you saved those on the ark through
    water.
After the flood you set in the clouds a rainbow.
When you saw your people as slaves in Egypt,
  you led them to freedom through the sea.
Their children you brought through the Jordan
  to the land which you promised.

Sing to the Lord all the earth.
Tell of his mercy each day.

In the fullness of time you sent Jesus,
  nurtured in the water of a womb.
He was baptized by John and anointed by your Spirit
  at the Jordan.
He called his disciples to share in the baptism
  of his death and resurrection,
  and to make disciples of all nations.

Declare his works to the nations,
His glory among all the people.

By the power of your Holy Spirit,
  bless this gift of water and those who receive it.

Wash away their sin and clothe them in righteousness as those who have died and been raised with Christ.

All praise to you, Eternal Father,
through your Son, Jesus Christ,
who with you and the Holy Spirit
lives and reigns forever. Amen.

ADMINISTRATION OF WATER BAPTISM AND LAYING ON OF HANDS

When there are no Baptisms, this section is omitted. As the water is administered, the minister says:

(Name), I baptize you in the name of the Father and of the Son and of the Holy Spirit. **Amen.**

As hands are placed on the heads of those receiving Baptism, the minister says:

The power of the Holy Spirit work within you, that being born of water and the Spirit you may be a faithful witness of Jesus Christ. **Amen.**

When all candidates have been baptized, the minister addresses them:

Through Baptism you are incorporated into Christ's New Creation by the power of the Holy Spirit and share in Christ's royal priesthood. With joy and thanksgiving we welcome you as *member(s)* of the universal body of Christ.

CONFIRMATION AND OTHER RENEWAL OF THE BAPTISMAL COVENANT

As the minister says the following words, water may be sprinkled toward all persons being confirmed or making other renewal of their baptismal faith.

Remember your Baptism and be thankful. **Amen.**

As hands are placed upon the head of each person separately, the minister says to each:

(Name), the power of the Holy Spirit work within you, that having been born of water and the Spirit, you may continue to be a faithful witness of Jesus Christ. **Amen.**

[PROFESSION OR RENEWAL OF FULL MEMBERSHIP IN THE UNITED METHODIST CHURCH

The minister asks those coming into full membership in this congregation of The United Methodist Church:

As *members* of Christ's universal church, will you be loyal to The United Methodist Church, participating in its mission by your prayers, your presence, your gifts, and your service; and as *members* of this congregation, will you do all in your power to effect fellowship and ministry in this community?

I will.]

[COMMENDATION AND WELCOME

For newly baptized and confirmed; omitted when only the renewal is enacted. The congregation is then addressed.

Members of the family of God, I commend to you *these persons.* Do all in your power to increase *their* faith, confirm *their* hope, and perfect *them* in love.

We give thanks to God
for the faith he has worked within you.
We pledge to you
our Christian love and hospitality
as fellow stewards of God's grace.
Together with you and all Christians
we seek the unity of the Spirit
in the bond of peace,

**that in everything God may be glorified
through Jesus Christ.]**

BAPTISMAL BLESSING
Almighty God,
who has give us new birth by water and the Holy Spirit,
and bestowed upon us the forgiveness of sins,
keep you in newness of life,
Through Jesus Christ our Lord.   **Amen. Alleluia!**

THE PEACE

4. Service of the Bread and Cup
(Easter Communion)

OFFERING   *See* Book of Hymns *438; also 318, 441,
443, and 451.*

TAKING OF THE BREAD AND CUP
*Here the table is prepared during the singing of the hymn.
The gifts of bread and wine are brought forward from the
congregation with the other gifts, or from a nearby table.
When the table is ready, the minister says:*

Beloved in Christ! People shall be gathered from north
and south, from east and west to feast at the heavenly
banquet of the Lord. Christ our Paschal Lamb has been
sacrificed. Let us therefore celebrate the feast. Alleluia!

GREAT THANKSGIVING
The Lord be with you.

And also with you.

Lift up your hearts.

We lift them to the Lord.

Let us give thanks to the Lord our God.

It is right to give him thanks and praise.

It is truly right to glorify you, Father, and to give you
thanks;
for you alone are God, living and true, dwelling in light
inaccessible from before time and for ever.

Fountain of life and source of all goodness, you made
all things and fill them with your blessing;
you created them to rejoice in the splendor of your
radiance.

Countless throngs of angels stand before you to serve you
night and day; and, beholding the glory of your presence,
they offer you unceasing praise. Joining with them,
and giving voice to every creature under heaven,
we acclaim you, and glorify your name, as we sing (say):

Holy, holy, holy Lord, God of power and might,
heaven and earth are full of your glory.
Hosanna in the highest.
Blessed is he who comes in the name of the Lord.
Hosanna in the highest.

We acclaim you, holy Lord, glorious in power.
Your mighty works reveal your wisdom and love.
You formed us in your own image, giving the whole
world
into our care, so that, in obedience to you, our
Creator,
we might rule and serve all your creatures.
When our disobedience took us far from you,
you did not abandon us to the power of death.
In your mercy you came to our help,
so that in seeking you we might find you.
Again and again you called us into covenant with you,
and through the prophets you taught us to hope for
salvation.

You loved the world so much that in the fullness of
time you sent your only Son to be our Savior.
Incarnate by the Holy Spirit, born of the Virgin Mary,
he lived as one of us, yet without sin.
To the poor he proclaimed the good news of salvation;
to prisoners, freedom; to the sorrowful, joy.
To fulfill your purpose he gave himself up to death;
   and, rising from the grave, destroyed death,
   and made the whole creation new.

That we might live no longer for ourselves
but for him who died and rose for us,
he sent the Holy Spirit,
his own first gift for those who believe,
to complete his work in the world,
and to bring to fulfillment the sanctification of all.

When the hour had come for him to be glorified
   by you, his heavenly Father,
having loved his own who were in the world,
he loved them to the end:
at supper with them he took bread,
and after giving you thanks,
he broke the bread, gave it to his disciples, and said:
"Take, eat; this is my body which is given for you.
Do this in remembrance of me."

When the supper was over,
he took the cup, gave thanks,
and gave it to his disciples, saying:
"Drink from this, all of you;
this is the cup of the new covenant in my blood,
poured out for you and the many,
for the forgiveness of sins."

The day you raised him from the dead
he was recognized by his disciples
at the breaking of the bread.

183

**[When we eat this bread and drink this cup,
we experience anew the presence of the Lord Jesus Christ
and look forward to his coming in final victory.]**

Father, we now celebrate this memorial of our
        redemption.
Recalling Christ's death and his descent among the dead,
proclaiming his resurrection and ascension to your right
        hand,
awaiting his coming in glory;
and offering to you from the gifts you have given us,
this bread and this cup,
we praise you and we bless you.

**We praise you, we bless you,
we give thanks to you,
and we pray to you, Lord our God.**

Lord, we pray that in your goodness and mercy
your Holy Spirit may descend upon us, and upon these
        gifts,
sanctifying them and showing them to be
holy gifts for your holy people,
the bread of life and the cup of salvation,
the Body and Blood of your Son Jesus Christ.

Grant that all who share this bread and cup
may become one body and one spirit,
a living sacrifice in Christ
to the praise of your Name.

Remember, Lord, your one holy catholic and apostolic
        church,
redeemed by the blood of your Christ.
Reveal its unity, guard its faith, and perfect it in your
        love.
Grant that we may find our inheritance with
all the saints who have found favor with you in ages past.

184

We praise you in union with them and give you glory through your Son Jesus Christ our Lord.

**Through Christ, and with Christ, and in Christ,
in the unity of the Holy Spirit,
all honor and glory are yours, Almighty God and Father,
for ever and ever.   Amen.**

As our Savior Christ has taught us, we are bold to pray:

LORD'S PRAYER   **Our Father ...** *All pray together.*

THE BREAKING OF BREAD

THE GIVING OF THE BREAD AND THE CUP
During the Communion, suitable hymns or joyous Easter anthems may be sung.

PRAYER AFTER COMMUNION
You have given yourself to us, Lord.

Now we give ourselves for others.

You have raised us with Christ, and made us a new people;

As a people of the resurrection, we will serve you with joy.

Your glory has filled our hearts;

Help us to glorify you in all things.   Amen.

HYMN or DOXOLOGICAL STANZA

DISMISSAL WITH BLESSING
Go in peace to love and serve the Lord.

We are sent in the power of Christ's resurrection. Alleluia!

The blessing of Almighty God,
Father, Son, and Holy Spirit,
is with you always. Amen.

Amen. Alleluia, alleluia!

Commentary

Because this service is the richest and most glorious occasion for worship in the entire year, great care must be taken in preparation for it. The key decision is whether to hold the great Easter Vigil at night, or to hold an early Sunday morning service. In either case, it is the first service of Easter, and may be celebrated at a suitable time between mid-evening on Saturday and sunrise Easter Sunday; and it should only be celebrated once. The mid- and late-morning services on Sunday are called the Resurrection of the Lord, or the Second Service of Easter. In several respects, the Saturday night time, beginning around 10:30 P.M. and ending just after midnight, is the most dramatic time. It may, of course, be held any time after nightfall. If, however, a night service is unrealistic for the majority of the congregation who wish to attend, then the early morning hour is fitting, provided that it begin in darkness. Either may be followed by a joyful Paschal breakfast.

A third option for celebrating the First Service of Easter may be considered in some circumstances. The service of the light and the service of the Word may be held through the reading of the Easter Gospel and the sermon. Then a hymn is sung, and the congregation may have breakfast together. At a suitable time, the liturgy resumes with the Baptism and Renewal, followed by the Easter Communion. This has an advantage of permitting a slightly later starting time, though still near dawn; and it permits those who prepare the breakfast to attend the second half of the

186

service. This option, of course, lessens the unity and full dramatic sweep of the whole liturgy. If either the second or third option is followed, ample preparation time must be allowed for the Second Service of Easter.

Recall again the four-fold structure of the Easter Vigil: (1) Service of the Light, (2) Service of the Word, (3) Service of the Water, or Baptism and Renewal, (4) Service of the Bread and Cup, or Easter Communion. In the Service of the Light, we carry forth an ancient Jewish practice which the primitive church inherited and gave a new significance. The *Lucernarium* (Service of the Lights) was done at nightfall at the beginning of vigils before the Lord's Day. Rooted in Jewish home ritual—the lighting of the lamps on Sabbath eve—it was discontinued in time, but maintained with special meaning in the Easter Vigil.

The kindling of the new fire can be done quite simply. It is best done outside in an ample container of metal, standing at last three feet high on strong supports. Dry wood arranged in a small "tent" shape on a covering of gravel or crushed stone in the base of the container works well. If done inside, a portable grate may be used, and a safe flammable substance, such as sterno, is useful in some instances. The container for the fire should express the dignity and simplicity of the action. Care should be taken to see that the fire is completely extinguished after the Paschal candle and other candles are lit and the procession begins. A smothering lid may be designed to place over the burning materials by an assistant after the celebrants leave the position of the fire.

During the procession, the celebrant or assistant, or a soloist or the choir, sings the "Light of Christ," and the congregation responds, singing, "Thanks be to God." Where a procession does not form outside, the choir and minister may process from the place of assembly or from the entranceway, pausing the three times indicated for the sung versicle and response.

If there is a congregational procession and the people are given individual candles, it is best to wait until the congregation has taken its place in the pews or seats before the candles are lighted. Designated persons or ushers will then light tapers from the Paschal candle and initiate the light at the end of each row. The congregation then holds the lighted candles throughout the *Exsultet,* at the conclusion of which they are extinguished.

The *Exsultet* is one of the great sung poetic treasures of the church. This ancient Paschal hymn is sung only once each year. The text given is suitable for traditional chanting by a song leader or soloist. There are three other possibilities as well, including variation in translations available. (1) The opening verses are treated as a responsory with the congregation. (2) The antiphon is sung by the congregation at various points in response to the choir or soloist. (3) A brief version with opening responsory is used. The traditional chant may be found in the Roman Sacramentary or in the *Holy Week Offices,* edited by Massey H. Shepherd, Jr., (Greenwich, Connecticut: The Seabury Press, 1958). For a different translation of the *Exsultet,* see the *Book of Common Prayer (Proposed)* (pp. 286-87) used in Option 1. Here are the three options.

OPTION 1.

Rejoice now, heavenly hosts and choirs of angels,
and let your trumpets shout Salvation
for the victory of our mighty King.

Rejoice and sing now, all the round earth,
bright with a glorious splendor,
for the darkness has been vanquished by our eternal
  King.

Rejoice and be glad now, Holy Church,
and let your holy courts, in radiant light,
resound with the praises of your people.

[All who stand near this marvelous and holy flame,
pray with me to God the Almighty
for the grace to sing the worthy praise of this great light;
through Jesus Christ his Son our Lord,
who lives and reigns with him,
in the unity of the Holy Spirit,
one God, for ever and ever.   **Amen.**

The Lord be with you.

And also with you.

Let us give thanks to the Lord our God.

It is right to give him thanks and praise.]

It is truly right and good, always and everywhere,
with our whole heart and mind and voice, to praise you,
the invisible, almighty, and eternal God, and your only-
begotten Son, Jesus Christ our Lord;
for he is the true Paschal Lamb, who at the feast of the
Passover paid for us the debt of Adam's sin,
and by his blood delivered your faithful people.

This is the night, when you brought our fathers,
the children of Israel, out of bondage in Egypt,
and led them through the Red Sea on dry land.
This is the night, when all who believe in Christ are
delivered from the gloom of sin, and are restored
    to grace and holiness of life.
This is the night, when Christ broke the bonds of death
    and hell, and rose victorious from the grave.

[How wonderful and beyond our knowing, O God, is
    your

mercy and loving-kindness to us,

that to redeem a slave, you gave a Son.

How holy is this night, when wickedness is put to flight,

and sin is washed away. It restores innocence to the fallen,

and joy to those who mourn. It casts out pride and hatred,

and brings peace and concord.

How blessed is this night, when earth and heaven are joined

and man is reconciled to God.]

Holy Father, accept our evening sacrifice,

the offering of this candle in your honor.

May it shine continually to drive away all darkness.

May Christ, the Morning Star who knows no setting,

find it ever burning—he who gives his light to all creation,

and who lives and reigns for ever and ever. **Amen.**

OPTION 2 Antiphon

(First sung by the choir, then all repeat; then all sing it each of the five times as a responsory. The congregation needs only the printed music for the antiphon.)

Re-joice, heav-en-ly pow-ers! Sing, choirs of an-gels!

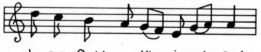

Je-sus Christ, our King is ri-sen!

I Choir:

Rejoice heavenly powers! Sing choirs of angels!
Exult, all creation around God's throne!
Jesus Christ, our King is risen!
Sound the trumpet of salvation!
Rejoice, O earth, in shining splendor,
radiant in the brightness of your King!
Christ has conquered! Glory fills you!
Darkness vanishes for ever!

Antiphon: *All sing.*
Rejoice, heavenly powers! Sing, choirs of angels!
Jesus Christ, our King is risen!

II Choir:

For Christ has ransomed us with his blood,
and paid for us the price of Adam's sin to our
    eternal Father!
This is our Passover feast, when Christ, the true Lamb,
is slain, whose blood consecrates the homes of all
    believers.
This is the night when first you saved our forebearers:
you freed the people of Israel from their slavery
and led them dry-shod through the sea.
This is the night when the pillar of fire destroyed
    the darkness of sin!
This is the night when Christians everywhere,
washed clean of sin and freed from all defilement,
are restored to grace and grow together in holiness.
This is the night when Jesus Christ broke the chains
of death and rose triumphant from the grave.

Antiphon: *All sing.*
Rejoice, heavenly powers! Sing, choirs of angels!
Jesus Christ, our King is risen!

III Choir:

What good would life have been to us,
had Christ not come as our Redeemer?
Father, how wonderful your care for us!
How boundless your merciful love!
To ransom a slave you gave away your Son.
O happy fault, O necessary sin of Adam,
which gained for us so great a Redeemer!
Most blessed of all nights, chosen by God to see
Christ rising from the dead!
Of this night Scripture says: "The night will
be clear as day: it will become my light, my joy."

Antiphon: *All sing.*
Rejoice, heavenly powers! Sing, choirs of angels!
Jesus Christ, our King is risen!

IV Choir:

The power of this holy day dispels all evil,
washes guilt away, restores lost innocence and
brings mourners joy.
Night truly blessed when heaven is wedded to earth
and man is reconciled with God!
Therefore, heavenly Father, in the joy of this night
receive our evening sacrifice of praise,
your church's solemn offering.

Antiphon: *All sing.*
Rejoice, heavenly powers! Sing, choirs of angels!
Jesus Christ, our King is risen!

V Choir:

Accept this Easter candle. May it always dispel
the darkness of this night!
May the Morning Star which never sets
find this flame still burning:
Christ, that Morning Star, who came back from the dead,

and shed his peaceful light on all mankind,
your Son who lives and reigns for ever and ever. Amen.

Antiphon: *All sing.*
Rejoice, heavenly powers! Sing, choirs of angels!
Jesus Christ, our King is risen!

(Note: The translation used above may employ the musical setting found in the Roman Catholic Liturgy of Holy Week, published by the Liturgical Press, Collegeville, Minnesota 56321. In some cases, church musicians may wish to compose new settings suitable for choir and congregation, as in Option 2.)

OPTION 3.
Rejoice, heavenly choirs of angels.

Rejoice, all creation around God's throne.

Jesus Christ, our King, is risen!

Sound the trumpet of salvation.

Rejoice, O earth, in shining splendor,

Radiant in the brightness of your King.

Christ has conquered! Glory fills you!

Darkness vanishes for ever.

This is our Passover feast when Christ,
    the true Lamb is slain,
    whose blood consecrates the homes of all believers.

This is the night when you, Lord our God,
    first saved our ancestors in the faith:
you delivered the people of Israel from their
    slavery and led them dry-shod through the sea.

This is the night when Christ broke the chains of
    death and rose triumphant from the grave.

This is the night truly blessed when heaven is
    wedded to earth,
and all creation is reconciled with God.

Therefore, Father, in the joy of this night,
receive our sacrifice of praise and thanksgiving.
Let us sing with joy,
joining the mighty chorus of all God's people!

HYMN   *See* Book of Hymns *437, 439, 443, or 451.*

or

Rejoice, heavenly choirs of angels.

Rejoice, all creation around God's throne.

Christ has conquered! Glory fills you!

Darkness vanishes for ever.

*Followed by hymn 493, verses 1 and 5; and the following
verses may be used between 1 and 5.*

O Christ, who art the Light and Day,
Thou drivest death and night away!
We know thee as the Light of light,
Illuminating mortal sight.

Teach us to live, that we may dread
The grave as little as our bed;
Teach us to die, that so we may
Rise glorious at the Judgment Day.

In some situations the order of the first two parts of the
liturgy may be reversed; following the vigil readings with
the Service of the Light. This is particularly suitable when
the new fire cannot take place outside the sanctuary, or
when the prayer vigil of Friday and Saturday continues up
until the beginning of the Easter Vigil itself.

In this case, the congregation assembles in the semi-darkness, joining those in the last of the "watch," with only a few small stationary lights or candles near the reading stand. After a brief introduction, the ministers enter in silence and take their places. In a small church, this may be done after the minister and choir are already in place. The readings from holy history continue up through the Epistle lection from Romans 6. At this time, the ministers move to the place where the new fire is to be kindled. The fire is lighted and the Paschal candle lit from it, and a procession forms, moving toward the front of the sanctuary again, singing "Christ our Light," with the congregational response. At each pause, other candles are lighted and, in turn, the congregation's individual candles, row by row. At the third response, when all are in position at the front, all the lights come on as the Paschal candle is placed in its holder, and the *Exsultet* is sung or recited. The celebrant then proclaims the Easter Gospel, in reading and in sermon. The Baptisms and Renewals then take place, followed by the Easter Communion, according to the pattern given above.

This arrangement allows a more austere vigil, though it does not allow the presence of the lighted Paschal candle, symbolizing the light of Christ, in the midst of the reading of holy history from Genesis through the prophets. This is a choice between a continuing vigil—with a more dramatic and close connection between the symbolism of light and the water of Baptism—and the more traditional ancient symbolism of the initial service of light and the new fire.

In the case of a continuing Friday-Saturday prayer vigil, the cross may be unveiled and the Easter paraments, banners, flowers, and other visuals placed during the final hour before the whole congregation assembles. Or, it may occur as the people process into the worship area. As people gather, they participate in the extended vigil; and, in some situations, witness the transformation of the church before moving into the readings.

The Service of the Word of God focuses upon the history of salvation and is fundamental to our participation in the Easter-Passover mystery. There are nine lections appointed, including the Epistle and Gospel. Throughout history the number has varied from as many as seventeen in some Eastern liturgies to as few as five. Unless there are serious reasons for not doing so, all or most of the Old Testament lections should be read. In any case, at least three of them should be read, including Genesis 1 and the Exodus 14 passage. The readings from the New Testament are, of course, essential.

The basic structure of this part of the liturgy consists in a lection, a psalm (or biblical canticle), followed by a brief collect form of prayer. This may be varied in a number of ways. For example, hymn verses may be subsituted for some of the psalms; or there may be readings followed by a brief silence, or by psalms, with one common prayer at the beginning of the whole series. Psalm 139 may be used as a common response throughout, with congregation reciting, "For God's steadfast love endures for ever." One or two of the verses may be used in response to each lection, followed by the congregational antiphon.

Once the basic dynamic and point of the reading of salvation history is understood, a great deal of creativity may be exercised in how the service of the Word is done. There is ample historical precedent, for example, in having various groups of readings done at different places or "stations"—both inside and outside the building. One can imagine beginning with the Genesis-Exodus readings then a short drama or media response, then a procession to another place for readings from the prophets, followed by a drama or nonbiblical reading; and finally, a movement back to the sanctuary for Romans 6 and the Easter Gospel.

196

If the circumstances of time and place permit such an elaboration (for example, in a college or university chapel), a special committee to work solely on the service of the Word should be formed well in advance.

Of course much simpler variations may also be done effectively with careful planning. For example, the Genesis-Exodus readings lend themselves well to a media presentation. A plain white reflective cloth may be brought in by two persons and held in place during slides interpreting the creation, then quietly removed by the same persons. This avoids setting up screens. The projectors may be unobtrusively placed in the pews or aisles and removed immediately after use.

After the last Old Testament lection, the "Glory to God in the Highest" may be sung, and church bells rung out, according to local custom. Or, this act of praise may follow after the Roman 6 reading, in which case Psalm 114 is quite fitting, especially when sung. A short sermon may follow any of the readings, or there may be a sermon following the reading of the Easter Gospel. In any case, these proclamations should be brief and powerfully to the point. Some may consider reading one of the beautiful patristic Easter sermons such as those of Saints John Chrysostom, Basil of Caesarea, or Gregory the Great. These are found in *The Awe-Inspiring Rites of Initiation.*[9]

Following the Easter Gospel and sermon, a brief silence may be kept. This provides a moment for assimilation and a pause before moving to the deep mystery of Christian initiation and the renewal of the congregation's baptismal promises. If this is an early Sunday morning service, and the Easter breakfast comes at this point (as in Option 3), a hymn may be sung in procession to the fellowship hall.

The Service of the Water, of Baptism and Renewal, proclaims in sign-actions the central fact of our rebirth and identity in Christ. Before any specific plans are made, the minister(s) and the worship planning committee should read *A Service of Baptism, Confirmation, and Renewal: An Alternate Text, 1976* and be familiar with its theology and usage. This is the basic rite which is employed in this section of the liturgy. Where there are no Baptisms, only the appropriate sections are used (Confirmation or Renewal of vows by the congregation).

Congregational renewal of the baptismal covenant should *never* be omitted, and should also occur at the Second Service of Easter whenever possible. Where only the Renewal occurs, water is sprinkled or cast toward the congregation from small hand-held evergreen boughs. Or, bowls of water may be poured out near the font and then carried through the congregation as the minister(s) sprinkle the water gently toward the people with a sweep of the hand, saying, "Remember your Baptism, and be thankful!" Lay persons may assist in these actions. Spontaneous responses, such as, "Amen," "Thanks be to God," or "Alleluia," are to be encouraged; and nonverbal signs such as lifting of the hands or making the sign of the cross are appropriate. Then, after the whole congregation has received the renewal sign of water, the minister(s) returns and pronounces the baptismal blessing.

In some churches a form of the litany of saints may be used in connection with the baptismal rite. Here are some possibilities, depending upon time and space, and the theological convictions of the congregation and ministers.

1. Following the brief introduction, "In this we enter the communion of saints . . . ," there may occur a *naming of the saints,* a proclaiming of a selected list beginning with Mary and the apostles, and including names through the centuries. For example: Mary and Martha, Benedict, Francis, Theresa, Martin Luther, John Wesley, Mary Bethune, Martin Luther King, and ending with "all holy men and women. In their company we pray to the Lord";

and the congregation responds, "Lord, have mercy," or, "Lord, save your people."

2. In the same pattern, naming persons of the particular local church, the congregation may then be led in specific bidding prayers. For further details see earlier commentary on "Prayers of the People," and *Word and Table,* p. 34.

3. A more elaborate form involves the list of saints by groups: martyrs, preachers and pastors, theologians, missionaries and evangelists, reformers and prophets of social justice, and "those faithful in obscurity." Each group would include saints from both ancient and modern periods. For example: (martyrs) Peter, Stephen, Paul, Perpetua, Polycarp, Thomas More, Michael Servetus, Joan of Arc, Dietrich Bonhoeffer, Martin Luther King; (preachers and pastors) Apostle Paul, Saint Francis, Lancelot Andrewes, John Wesley, Jonathan Edwards, Harry Emerson Fosdick; (prophets and workers for social justice) Harriet Tubman, Dag Hammerskjold, John Woolman, Walter Rauschenbush, Clara Barton, Rachel Carson; (artists, musicians, and writers) J. S. Bach, John Donne, Pearl S. Buck, John Milton, Michelangelo, Mahalia Jackson, John Bunyan, Rembrandt, Palestrina, Dante, Charles Wesley.

As each group is called, persons could stand to be identified with them, or process to a place near the baptimal font, if the space is ample. After all have gathered under a banner or other sign of each group, the prayers of the people are offered.

4. An alternate litany may be done, beginning with the responses, preferably sung:

Lord, have mercy	**Lord, have mercy.**
Christ have mercy	**Christ, have mercy.**
Lord, have mercy	**Lord, have mercy.**

Then the saints' names may be sung, followed again by responses:

Lord, be merciful	**Lord, save your people.**
From all evil	**Lord, save your people.**
From every sin	**Lord, save your people.**
From everlasting death	**Lord . . .**
By your incarnation	**Lord . . .**
By your death and rising to new life	**Lord . . .**
By the gift of your Holy Spirit	**Lord . . . Amen.**

Note that if the litany of the saints is used, prayers for the church may be better placed after the baptismal blessing. At that point, the peace may be given and signs of reconciliation and love are exchanged. This has the added advantage if there are adult Baptisms, of permitting them to participate in the prayers of the people and the Easter communion immediately after Baptism, as was the custom in the early church. If the font is not in the front of the sanctuary and there has been a procession to it, the hymn of preparation may be sung in procession back to the seats, during which time the table is prepared and the elements brought forward.

On this occasion the finest bread should be prepared. It is particularly significant if one of the families who has prepared it assists in bringing the gifts forward. In some churches, where an Easter breakfast will follow the service, it is a glorious custom to invite each household to bring breads of various sorts, some of which will be used for the Holy Communion. The remaining breads will be used at the breakfast. People of various folk and ethnic backgrounds bring their special breads, and other suitable foods, to be placed in containers at the church entrance. These, along with such items as fruits of various kinds, olives, honey, cheese, and eggs, may be then taken to the place where the breakfast is to be held.

The Great Thanksgiving for this liturgy is a slightly adapted version of "A Common Eucharistic Prayer,"[10] and is particularly well suited for this celebration because of its richness and universality. The presiding minister should be thoroughly familiar with it; for it should be prayed with grace and great joy. The people's responses should be sung with confidence and vigor, and should be learned ahead of time.

Throughout the service, particular care should be given to the musical settings of the texts, the hymn selection and the instrumental music used. Brass fanfares and instrumental variations on the hymn tunes can be most effective. The choir need not prepare special anthems for the Easter Vigil, but rather should concentrate on leading the congregational song. The Second Service of Easter is a better time for anthems or larger choral pieces, such as traditional selections from Handel's "Messiah" or contemporary forms. However, during the Communion, appropriate Easter Chorales and anthems may be sung by the choir if desired. Brass and choral work may resound at the conclusion of the service as well, continuing the great themes of the Paschal feast.

X.

Easter Sunday, or The Second Service of Easter: An Order of Worship with Commentary

GATHERING

Festive music, both instrumental and choral, may be offered during the gathering of the people. This music may include brass, and may begin ten to fifteen minutes before the normal time, particularly when there is one main Sunday service following the Easter Vigil or First Service of Easter. In some situations, the bringing in and placing of flowers may be done as an informal procession as various families and congregation members arrive.

GREETING

Christ is risen!

The Lord is risen indeed!

Glory and honor, dominion and power
   be to God for ever and ever.

Christ is risen! Alleluia!

HYMN OF PRAISE

Hymns 437, 439, 440, 443, 446, 448, and 452 are especially appropriate. If the hymn is to be an entrance song with procession, it precedes the greeting.

OPENING PRAYER

The Lord is with you.

And also with you.

Let us pray: *a brief pause*
O God, who for our redemption gave your only-begotten Son
   to the death of the cross,
   and by his glorious resurrection delivered us from
   the power of our enemy:
Grant us so to die daily to sin,
   that we may evermore live with him in the joy of
   his resurrection;
Through Jesus Christ your Son our Lord,
   who lives and reigns with you and the Holy Spirit,
   one God, now and for ever.   **Amen.**

or

God our Father,
   by raising Christ your Son,
   you conquered the power of death
   and opened to us the way to eternal life.
Let our celebration today
   raise us up and renew our lives
   by the Spirit that is within us.
Grant this through our Lord Jesus Christ,
   your Son, who lives and reigns with you
   and the Holy Spirit,
   one God, for ever and ever.   **Amen.**

FIRST LECTION
  Acts10:34-48
    or   (Year A: 1981, 1984, 1987)
  Exodus 14:10-14, 21-25; 15:20-21
  Isaiah 25:6-9
    or   (Year B: 1979, 1982, 1985)
  Acts 10:34-48
  Exodus 15:1-11
    or   (Year C: 1980, 1983, 1986)
  Acts 10:34-48

If the first lection is from the Old Testament, Acts 10:34-48
may be read as the second lection instead of the Epistle.

ACT OF PRAISE   Psalm 118:1-2, 14-24   (Years
                          A,B,C)

  Antiphon: **This is the day the Lord has made;**
            let us rejoice and be glad in it.

            Give thanks to the Lord, for he is good;
                his mercy endures for ever.
            Let Israel now proclaim,
                "His mercy endures for ever."

  Antiphon: **This is the day the Lord has made;**
            let us rejoice and be glad in it.

            The Lord is my strength and my song,
                and he has become my salvation.
            There is a sound of exultation and victory
                in the tents of the righteous:
            "The right hand of the Lord has triumphed!
            the right hand of the Lord is exalted!
            the right hand of the Lord has triumphed!"

  Antiphon: **This is the day the Lord has made,**
            let us rejoice and be glad in it.

204

I shall not die, but live,
and declare the works of the Lord.
The Lord has punished me sorely,
but he did not hand me over to death.

Antiphon

Open for me the gates of righteousness;
I will enter them;
I will offer thanks to the Lord.
"This is the gate of the Lord,
he who is righteous may enter."
I will give thanks to you, for you answered
me
and have become my salvation.

Antiphon

The stone which the builders rejected
has become the chief cornerstone.
This is the Lord's doing,
and it is marvelous in our eyes.
On this day the Lord has acted;
we will rejoice and be glad in it.

Antiphon: **This is the day the Lord has made;
let us rejoice and be glad in it.**

or

Hymn 592 or "Glory Be to God on High"

SECOND LECTION
  I Peter 1:3-9,   (Year A: 1981, 1984, 1987)
or Acts 10:34-48
  I John 5:1-6,   (Year B: 1979, 1982, 1985)
or Acts 10:34-48
  Revelation 1:4-19,   (Year C: 1980, 1983, 1986)
or Acts 10:34-48

HYMN OR ANTHEM

EASTER GOSPEL

John 20:1-18	(Year A,B,C)
or	
Matthew 28:1-10	(Year A: 1981, 1984, 1987)
Mark 16:1-8	(Year B: 1979, 1982, 1985)
Luke 24:1-35	(Year C: 1980, 1983, 1986)

SERMON

RESPONSES TO THE WORD

RENEWAL OF BAPTISMAL COVENANT
Use the texts of the rite as found on pp. 176-81 in the Easter Vigil; or as in A Service of Baptism, Confirmation, and Renewal: An Alternate Text, 1976.

PRAYERS OF THE PEOPLE

THE PEACE
By dying, Christ destroyed our death;
In rising, he restores our life;
In giving us his Spirit, he grants us peace.
The peace of the Lord be with you.

And also with you.

Signs and words of peace and reconciliation are exchanged among all, using words such as "He is risen," or "The peace of Christ be with you."

OFFERING
When the Lord's Supper is not celebrated, the service concludes after the presentation of the offering with the following prayers, a hymn, and dismissal with blessing:

PRAYER OF THANKSGIVING
Blessed are you, O Lord our God,
Creator and redeemer of the whole world;

from you we receive the gift of life,
and by your grace we have gifts to offer you.
Accept our offerings and our lives in praise and
    thanksgiving,
    through Jesus Christ our Lord,
    who brings us again from death to life,
    and holds forth the promise of your everlasting
    kingdom. **Amen.**
As Jesus has taught us, we are bold to pray:

LORD'S PRAYER   **Our Father . . .**

HYMN

DISMISSAL WITH BLESSING
Go forth in joy to love and serve God in all that you do.

We are sent in the name of the risen Christ.

Let us bless the Lord.

Thanks be to God. Alleluia!

May the God of peace who raised to life the great
Shepherd of the sheep, make us ready to do his will in
every good thing, through Jesus Christ, to whom be glory
for ever and ever.

Amen. Alleluia!

*   *   *
**   **   **

*If the Lord's Supper is celebrated, the table is prepared at
the offering, during which a hymn or anthem is sung.*

GREAT THANKSGIVING
The text for the Easter Vigil is used; see pp. 181-85.

BREAKING OF THE BREAD

GIVING THE BREAD AND THE CUP

[PRAYER AFTER COMMUNION
Lord,
we bless and praise you for nourishing us with
this Easter feast of redemption,
Fill us with your Spirit,
and make us living signs of your love;
Through Jesus Christ our Lord.   **Amen.**]

HYMN or DOXOLOGICAL STANZA

DISMISSAL WITH BLESSING
Go forth in joy to love and serve God in all that you do.

We are sent in the name of the risen Christ.

Let us bless the Lord.

Thanks be to God. Alleluia!

May the God of peace who raised to life the great
Shepherd of the sheep,
make us ready to do his will in every good thing,
through Jesus Christ, to whom be glory for ever and ever.

Amen. Alleluia!

Commentary

Easter Sunday morning is an occasion of great joy and
renewal. Even in churches which have not followed the full
Christian year, this is a day of many rituals and local
customs. In particular, people expect to hear the Easter
Gospel and special music, to sing the Easter hymns, and to
see the beautiful flowers and vestments (clothes). This
service is designed to give these expectations a substantial
framework and pattern; but also to heighten the Word of
God and the theological meaning of Paschal renewal—of
dying and rising with Jesus our Lord.

If the Easter Vigil or the morning First Service of Easter

is followed by a breakfast, thought should be given as to how the lilies and other flowers may be placed in the sanctuary, since not all of them could be positioned and still leave space for the various actions surrounding Baptism and Eucharist. Here is one suggestion: A group of persons may be responsible for arranging and placing the flowers and other visuals. As persons arrive they may present flowers (including lilies) brought from their homes. This may be done quite festively, yet without show. Banners, paraments, and other visuals may also be placed at this time. A genuine atmosphere of offering and sharing may be experienced. If this is done while special music is offered, it should be done quietly. The gifts of flowers will then be taken to the sick and shut-in following the service. Not only will this save the church the expense of filling the sanctuary, but it will link the beauty of Easter worship with acts of love and ministry. Care should be taken not to "over-load" the room. Varieties of flowers with several lilies can be more striking than huge banks of nothing but lilies.

Concerning the readings from Scripture, note that if the first lection is from the Old Testament (Exodus or Isaiah), then the reading from Acts 10 may be used in place of the appointed second lection. Careful consideration for preaching must be given to the interaction of the lections. Differing themes and accents can be brought out for the congregation with different combinations of lections. Note also the alternative possibilities in the Gospel lections as well.

The responses to the Word present many possibilities. A hymn of joyful response may be sung, or an anthem which lifts up a theme of the Easter Gospel and the sermon may be offered. This is an excellent occasion for hymn-anthems which involve both choir and congregation in dialogue. The affirmation of faith in one of the historic creeds is particularly appropriate this Sunday of all Sundays.

It is especially fitting that the congregation be invited to renew their baptismal covenant, since this is at the heart of Christian life and the Easter faith. The form of the apostolic creed is that of question and answer in the context of the rite of baptismal Renewal. Wherever possible, the thanksgiving over the water should be used along with the sign-action of sprinkling water toward the people.

We must frankly recognize that this raises serious pastoral questions concerning the number of persons attending Easter Sunday services who are infrequent worshipers, or whose faith is nominal at best. Care should be taken to let the congregation know by a note in the bulletin or by a simple remark that this rite is for those desiring to renew their baptismal promises. This does not coerce; yet it has a powerful symbolic meaning for increasing numbers of United Methodists. It is an evangelical witness in the deepest sense and has something of a "converting ordinance"—to use Wesley's phrase—about it. This renewal of baptismal covenant shows vividly the essentials of Easter faith: being incorporated into the death and resurrection of Jesus Christ and his body, the church.

If the Sacrament of the Lord's Supper is celebrated, it should continue the great joy expressed in the Easter Vigil. During the communing of the people, it is especially recommended that people receive standing, and preferably in a continuing movement, rather than in the lengthy series of table dismissals which accompany the customary Communion reception of the bread and cup. Here too is an occasion for the great Easter music to be sung. Where this is not possible, the congregation should sing Easter hymns or carols throughout the Communion Rite.

XI.

The First Week in Easter: Resources

The remainder of the first week of the Easter Season extends the celebration of the holy joy of Easter. Where there is a local custom of Sunday evening gatherings, a special meal could be planned, and the worship may be based upon the Emmaus road story from Luke 24:13-35. This lends itself to dramatic reading or to pantomime. Throughout the week special events may be held for the newly baptized and their families. Families in the congregation should be encouraged to read the post-resurrection passages at their evening meals, especially those in John's Gospel (20:19-25, 26-31; and chapter 21). You may find a daily set of Easter week lections in the *Proposed Book of Common Prayer* (p. 958). The Letter of I Peter may also be read throughout the week, divided as follows: 1:1-12, 1:22–2:10, 2:11-25, 3:1-17, 3:18–4:ll, and 4:12–5:14. The Easter responsory should echo throughout the week's devotions and prayer. "Christ is risen! Alleluia!" **"Christ is risen indeed! Alleluia!"** This could be said or sung at the beginning and ending of family prayer. Some of the following responsories may also be used at church gatherings or in homes.

I know you are looking for Jesus the crucified
He has been raised, just as he promised.
Come and see the place where he was laid.

This is the day the Lord has made. Alleluia!

He commissioned us to be witnesses
that he is the one set apart by God
as judge of the living and the dead.

**This is the day the Lord has made;
Let us rejoice and be glad. Alleluia!**

Since you have been raised up
in company with Christ,
be intent upon things above
rather than on things of earth.

**This is the day the Lord has made;
Let us rejoice and be glad;
Let us feast with joy in the risen Lord. Alleluia!**

*   *   *
**   **   **

I am the light of the world,
who enlightens every person that comes into the world.

**You are the fountain of life;
In your light we see light.**

You were once darkness, but now are light in the Lord.
Be children of light; do not walk in darkness,
but let your light shine.

**In your light we see light,
until the Daystar shines in our hearts.**

212

Put on the whole armor of light,
that your light may shine before the world.
Who follows me, has the light of life.

You are the fountain of life;
In your light we see light.
Let the light of your face shine upon us, Lord. Alleluia!

During the first week of Easter it is also fitting to hold a Seder if it was not done during Holy Week. This is particularly meaningful if the Jewish time of Passover falls during the week. In the next chapter a full text with commentary is provided.

The Paschal candle should remain in the front of the church throughout the entire Great Fifty Days, until the Day of Pentecost, and should be lighted each Lord's Day or for any other occasion of worship. After the Day of Pentecost, the Paschal candle is appropriately placed near the baptismal font. It is lighted at all subsequent Baptisms to signify the resurrection and at services of death and resurrection as well.

XII.

A Passover Meal (Seder) with Commentary

Introduction

Passover is unique among Jewish holidays in that it places great emphasis on home celebration. Although synagogue services are, indeed, a significant part of the Passover observance, it is at the family *Seder* (Say-der) that the essential nature of the festival is fulfilled.[11]

The Seder incorporates a joyful family dinner into the worship service. In traditional homes there is a Seder on each of the first two nights of the holiday; in reform homes there is generally a Seder on the first night only. The Passover observance is a time for family reunions; it is a time of warm hospitality, and there is often a guest or two at the Seder service. In many contemporary synagogues a community Seder for the congregational family is conducted.

The Hebrew word *Seder* means "order" or "formal arrangement." It refers to the progression of ceremony prescribed for the family table on Passover night. Many of the Passover rites are of great antiquity and go back to traditions preserved from the first and second temples, in ancient Palestine, where the Jewish people lived until the destruction of the second temple in the year 70 of the Christian era.

The Seder attunes the participants to the meaning of the Egyptian bondage and renews the joy in freedom and redemption which derives from the Exodus.

Although the Seder is rooted in the specific biblical experience of thirty-two centuries ago, it also reflects the sorrows and hopes of the intervening centuries—including the horrors of the Nazi holocaust and the sense of renewal felt in the dynamic life of the Jewish community in the State of Israel. In sum, the Seder is expressive of permanently relevant ethical insights, of a zest for living, and of an unquenchable faith in God, humanity, and life.

It is because the Seder represents a microcosm of Jewish historic experience that the theme of Zion, and the yearning for Zion and Jerusalem, is recurrent in the Seder service. The ancient Israelites were liberated from the bondage of Egypt for two great purposes: to receive the divine Torah at Mount Sinai, and to journey to a new life in the Promised Land. In this land—the Holy Land—the Bible was created, the Rabbinic structure of law, wisdom, and morality came into being. "If I forget thee, O Jerusalem, let my right hand forget its cunning," was the vow of the psalmist who wept by the waters of Babylon during the first Exile, in the year 586 before the Christian era.

The great pilgrimage festival of Passover, when thousands streamed into Jerusalem to join in the paschal offerings, is recalled at the Seder service. In one brief phrase, "Next year in Jerusalem!" the timeless bonds of the Jew to his spiritual homeland are emphasized.

The Haggadah (Ha-ga-dah) is the book of worship used at the Seder service. Haggadah means the "re-telling" or the "narration" of the Exodus story. It is a response to four passages of the Bible, which offer the following behest:

"And you must tell your son on that day saying, This is done because of what the Eternal One did for me when I left Egypt . . . you shall therefore keep this ordinance in its due season from year to year" (Exodus 13:8-10. See also Exodus 12:26, 13:14; Deuteronomy 6:20).

With the exception of the biblical passages, the oldest portions of the Haggadah are from the pre-Maccabean years of twenty-five centuries ago. By the time of the Christian era, the text of the Haggadah had received much of its present form.

The Haggadah includes not only the story of the Exodus and the order of the ceremonies to be observed at the Seder, but also a running commentary of prayer, legend, hymn, and explanation.

In sustaining the interest of children in the Passover story and in making them understand the significance of the miraculous deliverance from Egyptian servitude, the resourcefulness of generations of parents was put to the test. Impromptu interruption of the Seder for relevant questions about the story and ritual is traditional. However, a set of four prescribed questions, the *Mah Nishtanah,* is included in the Haggadah to be asked by the youngest child present at the ceremony; this is to insure that certain important explanations are made, whether or not the child's curiosity prompts him to ask his elder. The service includes playful melodies which are appealing to children and a game of forfeits concerned with the *afikomen.*

Order of the Seder Service

1. THE KIDDUSH

The first cup is filled and the leader and celebrants recite the following blessings:

Praised art Thou, O Eternal our God, Ruler of the universe, Creator of the fruit of the vine. Praised art Thou, Who has chosen us, exalted and sanctified us through Thy commandments. Out of Thy love, Thou hast given us appointed seasons for rejoicing, even this Festival of Unleavened Bread, the time of our freedom, a sacred remembrance of the departure from Egypt. Praised art Thou, O Eternal, Who sanctifies Israel and the festive seasons, Who has preserved us, and sustained us, and brought us to this season.

The celebrants drink the first cup of wine.

2. THE HANDS WASHED

*Pitcher, basin, and towels are brought round
to each celebrant.*

3. THE GREENS EATEN

*The leader takes the parsley, lettuce, or watercress
from the Seder plate
and distributes it to the celebrants.
They dip the greens in salt water and say in unison:*

Praised be Thou, O Eternal our God, Ruler of the universe, Creator of the fruit of the earth.

The greens are then eaten.

4. THE AFIKOMEN

*The leader breaks the middle matzah,
leaving one-half on the Seder plate.
The other half, the afikomen, is hidden and will be eaten
at the end of the meal.*

5. THE PASSOVER STORY RECITED

"THIS IS THE BREAD OF AFFLICTION"

The leader uncovers the matzah on the Seder plate.
He lifts it up for all to see, and the company recites together.

This is the bread of affliction which our ancestors ate in the land of Egypt. Let all who are hungry enter and eat. Let all who are in want come and celebrate the Passover with us. This year we are here; next year in Jerusalem. Yesterday we were slaves, today we are free.

The matzah is set down. Wine is poured for the second cup.

"MAH NISHTANAH"—THE FOUR QUESTIONS

The youngest person at the Seder table
asks the four questions.

Why is this night different from all other nights?
—On all other nights, we eat either leavened or unleavened bread;
Why, on this night, only unleavened bread?
—On all other nights, we eat all kinds of herbs;
Why, on this night, bitter herbs especially?
—On all other nights, we need not dip herbs at all;
Why, on this night, do we dip them twice?

(The greens are dipped in salt water; i.e.,
the maror *is dipped in* haroset.*)*

—On all other nights, we may sit at the table either erect or reclining;
Why, on this night, do we recline?

"WE WERE THE SLAVES OF PHARAOH IN EGYPT"

The leader and the celebrants read the narrative,
either individually or in unison.

We were the slaves of Pharaoh in Egypt, and the Eternal our God, brought us forth from there with a mighty hand and an outstretched arm. And if the Holy One, Blessed be He, had not liberated our fathers from Egypt, then we, and our children, and our children's children, would have remained slaves to Pharaoh in Egypt. And so, even if we were all wise men, full of understanding, and deeply versed in the Torah, it would still be our duty from year to year to tell the story of the deliverance from Egypt. Indeed, praiseworthy is he who dwells on the deliverance from Egypt at length.

A STORY

It is told of five Palestinian scholars of ancient days, who once celebrated the Passover in the village of B'nai Brak. They kept discussing the story of the Exodus all through the night, so that before they knew it, it was dawn, and their students had to break in on them and remind them, "It is time to recite the morning prayer!"

THE FOUR SONS

The ancient Rabbis found, in Hebrew Scriptures,
four different versions of the command that the father tell
the story of the Exodus to his child.
From this they deduced that there were four different kinds
of children.

The Torah speaks about four sons; the wise one, the irreverent one, the one who is simple, and the one who does not know how to ask a question.

The wise child, eager to learn and to understand, asks, "What are the decrees, the statutes, and the laws which the Eternal our God commanded concerning Passover?" You should answer him in the spirit of his question, and explain to him the beautiful customs and observances of the festival.

The scornful, irreverent child asks, "What does this service mean to *you*?"—as though he were an outsider denying his kinship with his people. He should be scolded and told, "If *you* had been in Egypt, you would not have deserved to go forth to freedom."

The simple child is naive and shy. Though he would like to know what Passover means, he cannot find words beyond, "What is this all about?" He should be told, "With a strong hand, the Eternal brought us forth from Egypt, out of the house of bondage."

The fourth child cannot even phrase a question. You must tell him very simply, as the Torah puts it, "This (pointing to the matzah and the bitter herb) is because of what the Eternal did for me when I went forth from Egypt."

THE EGYPTIAN OPPRESSION

Praised is He Who is faithful to His promise to Israel, for He set a term to our bondage, fulfilling the word which He gave our father Abraham in the solemn covenant of the divided sacrifice, as it is written, "Be certain of this: your descendants shall reside in a land not their own, in subjection to people who will treat them harshly for four hundred years; but I shall punish the nation that held them in slavery, and then they shall get away with ample possessions" *(Genesis 15:13).*

This promise, which has stood by our forefathers, stands by us; for it was not only one tyrant who planned our destruction; but in every generation men have sought to destroy us, and the Holy One, Blessed be He, has delivered us from their hands.

"My father was a wandering Aramean, and he went down to Egypt, and sojourned there, few in number; and there he became a nation, great, mighty, and numerous"

(Deut. 26:5). Interpret this so: Jacob went to Egypt compelled by the Divine decree; it was never Jacob's intention to settle there permanently; during their long residence in Egypt, the Israelites retained their distinctive names, faith, and language.

"And the Egyptians dealt harshly with us, and oppressed us, and enslaved us in hard bondage" *(Deut. 26:6).* As it is written, "And the Egyptians said: 'Come, let us outwit them, lest they grow in number; for war may come, and they may join our enemies and fight against us, and thus leave our land' . . . and they set taskmasters over them, to torment them with heavy loads; and they built the treasure cities of Pithom and Ramses for Pharaoh . . . and the Egyptians drove the children of Israel ruthlessly at their task" *(Exodus 1:10, 11, 13).*

"And we cried unto the Eternal One, the God of our fathers, and He heard our voice, and saw our affliction, and our toil and our oppression" *(Deut. 26:7).* As Scripture tells us, "And in the course of those long years the king of Egypt died; and the children of Israel sighed in the midst of their slavery, and wept; and their cry came up to God from their bondage. And God heard their groaning, and He remembered His covenant with Abraham, with Isaac and with Jacob" *(Exodus 2:23, 24).*

"And the Eternal One brought us forth out of Egypt with a mighty hand, and with an outstretched arm, and with awesome terrors, and with signs, and with wonders" *(Deut. 26:8).* He sent no intermediary; it was God Himself, blessed be He, in His glory.

These are the ten plagues which the Holy One, blessed be He, visited upon the Egyptians in Egypt:

Each celebrant spills out a drop of wine from the cup
at the mention of each of the plagues,
as a symbol of regret that the victory had to be purchased

221

*through misfortune visited upon God's creations,
the Egyptians.*

Blood, Frogs, Lice, Beasts, Blight, Boils, Hail, Locusts, Darkness, Slaying of the First-Born.

(Here may be sung "The Dayenu," a traditional Passover Song: "If God had brought us out of Egypt. . . . Da-ye-nu.") Various musical settings are available. Write the Section on Worship, PO Box 840, Nashville, Tennessee 37202, or consult a local Jewish community.

THE PASSOVER SYMBOLS

The remembrance of the Exodus of our fathers from Egypt will never fail to inspire us with new courage, and the symbols of this festival always help to strengthen our faith in God, Redeemer of the oppressed. Thus our ancient teacher Rabban Gamaliel taught: "Whoever does not well consider the meaning of these three symbols: the Passover sacrifice, the matzah, and the bitter herb, has not properly observed this festival."

The leader holds up the shankbone, and says:

This shankbone, symbol of the Passover sacrifice, reminds us how the Holy One, blessed be He, passed over the houses of our forefathers in Egypt, "smiting the Egyptians and sparing us."

The leader points to the matzah.

This matzah reminds us how, in the haste of their departure from Egypt, our forefathers had to take along unleavened dough, "for they had not made any provisions for the road."

The leader points to the bitter herb.

222

This bitter herb reminds us how the Egyptians made bitter the lives of our forefathers in Egypt.

IN EACH GENERATION

In each generation, every man is duty-bound to envision himself as though he personally took part in the Exodus from Egypt; as we read in the Torah: "You shall tell your son on that day, saying, 'It is because of what the Eternal did for *me* when I came forth from Egypt.' " It was not only our forefathers that the Holy One, blessed be He, redeemed; He redeemed us, the living, together with them.

The celebrants join the leader in raising their wine-cups, and all recite:

We should therefore sing praises and give thanks and pour out infinite adoration to Him Who performed all these wonders for our fathers and for us. He brought us from slavery to freedom, from anguish to joy, from mourning to festivity, from darkness to light, and from bondage to redemption; and we will sing unto Him a new song, Halleluyah!

The benediction over the wine is recited; the assembled drink the second cup.

6. THE HANDS WASHED

The celebrants recite the following benediction.

Praised art Thou, O Eternal our God, Ruler of the universe, Who sanctified us with His commandments, and commanded us concerning the washing of the hands.

7, 8. THE BLESSINGS OVER THE MATZAH

A piece of matzah is distributed to each celebrant. All join in reciting the benediction, after which the matzah is eaten.

Praised art Thou, O Eternal our God, Ruler of the universe, Who brings forth bread from the earth.

Praised art Thou, O Eternal our God, Ruler of the universe, Who has sanctified us with His commandments, and commanded us concerning the eating of the matzah.

9. THE BITTER HERBS

*The leader distributes a piece of bitter herb to each celebrant;
the herb is dipped in* haroset, *and is eaten,
after reciting the following blessing.*

Praised art Thou, O Eternal our God, Ruler of the universe, Who has sanctified us with His commandments, and commanded us concerning the eating of the bitter herb.

10. THE HILLEL SANDWICH—
A REMINDER OF THE TEMPLE DAYS

*The leader distributes pieces of matzah
together with a fragment of bitter herb.
The celebrants eat them together,
first reciting this passage.*

Thus did Hillel do when the Temple in Jerusalem was still standing. He would put together a piece of the Paschal offering, a piece of matzah, and a piece of bitter herb, and eat them as one, in order literally to fulfill the biblical commandment, "With unleavened bread and bitter herbs shall they eat the Paschal lamb" *(Exodus 12:8).*

11. THE MEAL IS SERVED

12. THE AFIKOMEN

*At the meal's conclusion,
the children are given an opportunity
to find the concealed* afikomen.

After the leader redeems it,
and all partake of it, it is customary to eat nothing else.

13. GRACE AFTER THE MEAL

A brief segment of the blessings appears here.

Leader:	Let us say grace.
Company:	May the name of the Eternal be praised henceforth and forever.
Leader:	We will praise our God of Whose bounty we have partaken.
Company:	Praised is He of Whose bounty we have partaken, and through Whose goodness we live. Praised art Thou, O Eternal our God, Ruler of the universe, Who nourishes the whole world in goodness, grace, loving kindness, and compassion. "He gives food to all flesh, for His mercy is everlasting." Because of His enduring goodness, we have not lacked sustenance, and may we not lack it in the future—this for His great name's sake. For He is the universal Nourisher and Provider, beneficent toward all, and preparing sustenance for all living things of His creation. Praised art Thou, O Eternal, Who provides food for all.
Leader:	Our God and God of our fathers, be Thou ever mindful of us, as Thou has been of our fathers, so that we may find enlargement, grace, mercy, life, and peace on this Feast of Unleavened Bread.
Company:	Amen.
Leader:	Remember us this day in kindness.
Company:	Amen.
Leader:	Visit us this day with blessing.

Company:	Amen.
Leader:	O give thanks unto the Eternal, for He is good, for His mercy endures forever.
Company:	Thou openest Thy hand and satisfiest every living thing with favor.
Leader:	Blessed is the man who trusts in the Eternal; the Eternal will be unto him for a help.
Company:	The Eternal will give strength unto His people; He will bless His people with peace.

After the benediction over the wine,
all assembled partake of the third cup of wine.

THE CUP OF ELIJAH

The Cup of Elijah, which is set in the center of the table,
is now filled with wine.
The door of the house is opened.
The company rises as if to greet the prophet Elijah,
the long-expected messenger of
the final redemption of mankind from all oppression.
The Seder Ritual of Remembrance is read in unison:

On this night of the Seder we remember with reverence and love the six millions of [our] Jewish people of the European exile who perished at the hands of a tyrant more wicked than the Pharaoh who enslaved our fathers in Egypt. Come, said he, to his minions, let us cut them off from being a people, that the name of Israel may be remembered no more. And they slew the blameless and pure, men and women and little ones, with vapors of poison and burned them with fire. But we abstain from dwelling on the deeds of the evil ones lest we defame the image of God in which we were created.

Now, the remnants of our people who were left in the

226

ghettos and camps of annihilation rose up against the wicked ones for the sanctification of the Name, and slew many of them before they died. On the first day of Passover the remnants in the Ghetto of Warsaw rose up against the adversary, even as in the days of Judah the Maccabbee. They were lovely and pleasant in their lives, and in their death they were not divided, and they brought redemption to the name of Israel through all the world.

And from the depths of their affliction the martyrs lifted their voices in a song of faith in the coming of the Messiah, when justice and brotherhood will reign among mankind. "I believe with perfect faith in the coming of the Messiah: And though he tarry, nonetheless do I believe!" (from "Seder Ritual of Remembrance," by Rufus Learsi).

14. THE PSALMS OF PRAISE

The fourth and final cup of wine is filled.
The leader and company alternate in reciting the psalms,
a fragment of which is presented here.

When in straits, I called upon the Eternal; He answered me and set me free.

The Eternal is for me, I will not fear; What can man do unto me?

I was sore beset, about to fall, but the Eternal helped me.

The Eternal is my strength and my song, and He is become my deliverance.

I shall not die, but live, and recount the deeds of the Eternal.

The Eternal has indeed chastened me, but He has not given me over unto death.

Open to me the gates of victory; I will enter them, I will give thanks unto the Eternal.

This is the gate of the Eternal, the righteous shall enter it.

The breath of all the living shall acclaim Thy name, O eternal our God, and the spirit of all creatures shall ever glorify and exalt Thee, O our King. From everlasting to everlasting Thou art God, and beside Thee we have no king who redeems and delivers and sustains, and who in all times of trouble shows compassion. In truth, we have no sovereign but Thee.

After the blessing over the wine,
the celebrants partake of the fourth and final cup.
The celebrants read in unison.

Praised be Thou, O Eternal our God, Ruler of the Universe, for the vine and for the fruit of the vine, and for the produce of the field and for the goodly and pleasant land which Thou was pleased to give as an inheritance to our fathers. O Eternal our God, let Thy compassion pour out on Thy people, on Jerusalem, Thy city, and on Zion, the abode of Thy glory.

It is customary at this point in the service
for those present to join in the singing of Passover melodies,
which are to be found in most Haggadah texts.

15. CLOSING PRAYER

All assembled read together.

Our Passover Service is completed. We have reverently repeated its ordered tradition. With songs of praise we have called upon the name of God. May He Who broke Pharaoh's yoke, forever shatter all fetters of oppression, and hasten the day when war will be no more. Soon may He bring redemption to all mankind—freed from violence and from wrong, and united in an eternal covenant of brotherhood.

"Next year in Jerusalem!"

Commentary

The traditional *Seder* table is made as attractive as possible, with lighted festival candles, flowers, the finest linens and silver, and the following Passover symbols:

The Seder *plate* is placed at the head of the table near the leader of the Seder. Arranged on it are:

A roasted shankbone—a reminder of the Paschal Lamb.

A roasted egg—a symbol of the Festival sacrifice offered up in the Jerusalem Temple.

Maror (Mah-rir)—these bitter herbs (horseradish) are a reminder of the bitterness of the Egyptian slavery.

Haroset (Ha-roe-set)—a mixture of apples, nuts, cinnamon, and wine, which represents the mortar the Israelite slaves used in Egypt.

Parsley (or another green herb such as watercress or lettuce)—this is dipped into a *dish of salt water* before being eaten, which is symbolic of the coming of spring and the perpetual renewal of life.

Three matzahs—in commemoration of the unleavened bread which the Jews took with them when they fled Egypt.

Four cups of wine—the drinking of wine by each participant at four points in the Seder service symbolizes the four-fold promise of redemption in Exodus 6:6-7.

Cup of Elijah—This is usually a tall goblet which is placed in the center of the table. It is filled midway through the Seder.

A cushioned armchair for the leader, or a pillow placed on his chair. This symbolizes the freedom enjoyed by the Israelites when they are redeemed from bondage. In ancient times only free men could enjoy the comfort of leisurely dining.

Afikomen (Ah-fee-koh-men) or *dessert*. One of the three matzahs is broken in half. The half which is put away to be eaten at the close of the meal is called the *afikomen*. After it is distributed and eaten, no other food is taken. One of the customs connected with the *afikomen* is a game of paying forfeits. The leader good-naturedly takes no note of the spiriting away of the hidden matzah by the children. They do not surrender the *afikomen* until the leader redeems it with a gift or a promise of a gift.

The fifteen principal steps of the Seder ceremony are outlined by fifteen key Hebrew words, translated below. This easily memorized progression, which grew up in the course of centuries, has been put to music and is often sung by the Seder celebrants just before the service begins.

These words are addressed in the imperative to the leader.

Recite the Kiddush—blessings over the wine to consecrate the festival.

Wash the hands—prior to partaking of the green herbs.

Partake of the green herbs.

Divide the matzah—so that the *afikomen* may be put away.

Read the Haggadah.

Wash the hands for the meal proper.

Recite the two blessings over the matzah.

Recite the blessing over bitter herbs.

Eat the Hillel sandwich.

Serve the meal.

Eat the afikomen.

Say the Grace after meals.

Conclude the Hallel Psalms (The Psalms of Praise, Pss. 113–18).

Pray that God will accept your Seder service with favor.

XIII.

Ascension Day:
An Order of Worship
with Commentary

Introduction

With Easter evening begins the period of time known as the Great Fifty Days (see chapter 1, and the introductory chapter of *Seasons of the Gospel* for theological and pastoral meanings of this period). This is the season of the Spirit, since the Resurrection, the Ascension, and the Giving of the Holy Spirit are intimately linked in our confession of faith in Jesus Christ as Lord. The Scripture readings for this season are nearly breathless with excitement, surprise, and great vitality. The resurrection appearances follow one upon another with great mystery and power. The Lord's Day services should reflect and express this vivid sense of the presence of the risen Lord and the power of his gifts to those who love him. It is therefore a most fitting time for special musical events, festivals of gifts, and for fellowship meals which give opportunity for response to our great commissioning and to the range of gifts bestowed for ministry.

The church has traditionally marked the biblical reality of the ascension of the Lord who now "sits at the right hand of the Father," with a special feast. This day marks the rightful assumption of glory and power by the crucified one. While we mark the fortieth day of the Easter season, or the sixth Thursday, this is not merely an historical commemoration of the forty days of Jesus' post-resurrection life with his disciples, but rather a highlighting of an integral part of the Easter event according to the earliest traditions. In some churches it is not feasible to hold a special service on Thursday, in which case it may be celebrated the following Sunday, the seventh Sunday of Easter-Pentecost. This liturgy should make abundantly clear the connection between resurrection and ascension: Christ died and rose that we might have eternal life; and he ascended that we might be given a share in his divinity, his continuing presence, and hence, life with God. A careful study of all the lections of this season leading up to the ascension texts is essential to any planning. This biblical understanding will help avoid a shallow interpretation of the "event" of ascension.

GATHERING   *Suitable Ascension Day music may be offered.*

GREETING

Risen with Christ, let us seek the realities of the Spirit.

Our life is hidden with Christ in God.

He who descended is also ascended far above the heavens,

That he might fill all things.

When Christ, our Life appears,

We shall appear with him in glory! Alleluia!

HYMN   *See* Book of Hymns *74, 76, 453, 546, 547, and 458.*

OPENING PRAYER
The risen Christ is with you.

And also with you.

Let us pray: *A brief pause.*
Almighty God,
   whose blessed Son our Savior ascended far above all
   heavens that he might fill all things:
Mercifully grant us faith to recognize his abiding
   presence with his people on earth,
   even to the end of the ages;
Through Jesus Christ our Lord, who lives and reigns with
   you and the Holy Spirit, one God, in glory for ever.
Amen.

or

Ever-loving God,
Your only Son was taken up into heaven
   that he might prepare a place for us
and bestow the Spirit of Truth.
Make us joyful in his ascension
   so that we might worship him in his glory;
[Through Jesus Christ our Lord.   **Amen.**]
Illumine our hearts and minds by the power of the
Holy Spirit, that the Scriptures may be the living
Word to us this day.
Through Jesus Christ, our Lord.   **Amen.**

FIRST LECTION
Acts 1:1-11	(Years A,B,C)
or	
Daniel 7:9-14	(Year A: 1981, 1984, 1987)
Ezekiel 1:3-5*a*,	(Year B: 1979, 1982, 1985)
15-22, 26-28	
II Kings 2:1-15	(Year C: 1980, 1983, 1986)

(Note: Acts 1:1-11 may be used as a second lection when an Old Testament lection is used as the first lection.)

PSALM or ANTHEM   Psalm 110
  Antiphon: **The Lord will rule over the nations.**
    The Lord said to my Lord, "Sit at my right hand,
      until I make your enemies your footstool."
    The Lord will send the scepter of your power out of
      Zion,
      saying, "Rule over your enemies round about you.
    Princely state has been yours from the day of your
      birth;
      in the beauty of holiness have I begotten you,
      like dew from the womb of the morning."
  Antiphon: **The Lord will rule over the nation.**
    The Lord has sworn and he will not recant:
      "You are a priest for ever after the order of
      Melchizedek."
    The Lord who is at your right hand
      will smite kings in the day of his wrath;
      he will rule over the nations.
  Antiphon: **The Lord will rule over the nations.**

SECOND LECTION
  Ephesians 1:15-23 or Acts 1:1-11   (Years A,B,C)

HYMN or ANTHEM

GOSPEL
  Matthew 28:16-20   (Year A: 1981, 1984, 1987)
  Mark 16:9-20   (Year B: 1979, 1982, 1985)
  Luke 24:44-53   (Year C: 1980, 1983, 1986)

RESPONSE TO THE WORD

PRAYERS OF THE PEOPLE
  To each petition responding: **King of glory, hear our prayer.**

THE PEACE

OFFERING

If the Sacrament of the Lord's Supper is not celebrated, the service may conclude with the following prayers, a hymn, and the dismissal with blessing.

PRAYER OF THANKSGIVING

Let us pray: *A brief pause.*

Blessed are you, God and Father of our Lord Jesus Christ!

By your mercy we have been born anew to a living hope:
As once you brought your people through the Red Sea waters,

so from the waters of death you raise us to life with Christ;

Once we were no people, but now we are your people.

Help us grow as people of your new covenant
toward the fullness of the life our Savior bestows.

Accept these gifts and our lives,
that we may live always in the Spirit you share with Jesus Christ, in whom and through whom we pray.
Amen.

LORD'S PRAYER

HYMN

DISMISSAL WITH BLESSING

Go in the peace of Christ
to serve God and your neighbor.

We are sent in the name of the risen and glorified Lord.

May the blessing of Almighty God, the Father, Son, and Holy Spirit,
be with you now and for ever. **Amen. Alleluia!**

** ** **

When the Lord's Supper is celebrated, the table may be prepared and the gifts offered during the singing of the hymn or a suitable anthem.

GREAT THANKSGIVING
The Lord be with you.

And also with you.

Lift up your hearts.

We lift them to the Lord.

Let us give thanks to the Lord our God.

It is right to give him thanks and praise.

It is truly right to glorify you, Father Almighty,
on this day of ascending glory and praise.
You alone are the true and living God
  who created form from the void,
  light from the darkness,
  and life from the dust of the earth.
Even when we turned away from your goodness,
your mercy was not turned aside.
You gave us hope and made covenant,
delivered us from slavery, and set before us
  the way of righteousness and life.
The joy of life restored renews the face of the earth;
Therefore we join your whole family everywhere
in heaven and on earth,
in singing your unending praise:

Holy, holy, holy Lord, God of power and might.
Heaven and earth are full of your glory.
Hosanna in the highest.
Blessed is he who comes in the name of the Lord.
Hosanna in the highest.

Above all, loving God, we thank you that
you gave your Son Jesus Christ
   to save us and bring us home to you.
He proclaimed good news to the poor,
   release to the captives,
   he restored sight to the blind,
   and gave freedom to the oppressed.
He gave himself over to death
that we might be spared unending death.
You raised him up that we might live no longer
   for ourselves,
He ascended and sent the Holy Spirit
   to complete his work in the world
   and to bring to fulfillment the sanctification of all.

The night he gave himself up for us,
he took bread, gave thanks, broke it,
gave it to his disciples, and said:
"Take, eat, this is my body which is given for you."
When supper was over,
he took the cup, gave thanks, gave it to his disciples,
and said: "Drink from this, all of you;
this is my blood, which seals God's promise,
poured out for you and the many,
for the forgiveness of sins."

The day you raised him from the dead
he was recognized by his disciples
at the breaking of the bread.
He ascended to prepare a place for us
at your table in the Kingdom of life.

When we eat this bread and drink from this cup
we encounter anew the Lord Jesus Christ
and look forward to his coming in final victory.

Dying, you destroyed our death.
Rising, you restored our life.
Lord Jesus, come in glory!
Remembering his death and resurrection,
his ascension and his promise to be with us always,
we pray that the power of your Holy Spirit come
upon us and these gifts.
May the sharing of this bread and wine
be for us a participation in the body and blood of Christ.
May this sacrifice of praise and thanksgiving
in union with your Son's offering for us,
be a holy and acceptable giving of ourselves.
Make us one body in Christ,
that we may dwell with him and he in us,
and worthily serve you in this world.

Through him, with him, and in him,
in the unity of the Holy Spirit,
all glory and honor is yours, almighty God,
now and forever. Amen.

As Jesus has taught us, we are bold to say:

LORD'S PRAYER   **Our Father . . .**   *All pray*
together.

BREAKING OF THE BREAD

GIVING OF BREAD AND THE CUP

During the Communion appropriate hymns are sung.

[PRAYER AFTER COMMUNION
Lord,
We thank you for allowing us to share this Sacrament,
in the joy and power of the Holy Spirit;
Bind us to Christ, and fill us with your grace,
that we may be one in faithful service;
Through Jesus Christ our Lord.   **Amen.]**

HYMN or DOXOLOGICAL STANZA

DISMISSAL WITH BLESSING
Go in the peace of Christ to serve God and your
neighbor.

We are sent in the name of the risen and glorified Lord.

May the blessing of Almighty God, the Father, Son, and
Holy Spirit,
be upon you now and for ever.

Amen. Alleluia!

Commentary

If this service is celebrated on Thursday evening, it may
be held in connection with a congregational supper. The
theme of the gathering could center upon the meaning of
"Christ filling all things." The ascension theme could be
carried out in a number of ways. Presentations centering
upon key scriptural images, both as dramatizations and as
media events, might be given. (1) Christ is seated at the
right hand of the Father in victory; (2) "All authority in
heaven and on earth has been given to me"; (3) "Lo, I am
with you always, even to the end of the age"; (4) "It is to
your advantage that I go away"—"I will send the
Counselor, the Spirit of Truth, to you"; (5) "You shall
receive power when the Holy Spirit has come upon you,
and you shall be my witnesses . . . to the end of the earth;"
(6) "Why do you stand, gazing into heaven?"

This evening presents a good time to reflect together on
the meaning for the concrete life of the church today of
Christ's promise to be with us in witness and mission. Thus
a presentation or discussion of specific forms of the church's
witness and mission in the community might also form the
focus of the gathering. Worship could proceed the meal.

This might allow for a movement following Communion in an informal procession to a fellowship room from the sanctuary.

The same themes mentioned above form the basis of the prayers of the people (intercessions), and most certainly the sermon. These images also suggest the possibility of a simple media presentation in the context of the service, as part of the response to the Word, or in combination with the verbal proclamation. In general, the atmosphere of our worship on this occasion should be a joyful solemnity. There is at the heart of this feast, a profound mystery which cannot be expressed by mere hilarity and balloons, though the release of helium-filled balloons containing messages of the witness and mission of the gospel may be a suitable sign-act, and a way of involving children for example.

The visual experience of the sanctuary and the fellowship hall should be of strong vertical lines and simple, bold colors: white, gold, purple, and red. The quality of Ascension Day and its meaning is beautifully expressed in the following prayer from the *Verona Sacramentary*.

Rightly do we exult and rejoice on today's feast. The ascension into heaven of Jesus Christ, Mediator between God and man, is not an abandonment of us to our lowly state, for he exists now in the glory that he always had with you and in the nature he took from us and made his own. He deigned to become a man, in order that he might make us sharers in his divinity.[12]

"Christ enthroned in glory" opens up several strong visual possibilities, including the use of Pantocrater iconography.

When the Ascension is celebrated on the following Sunday, these same themes should be considered. It is crucial that the entire Great Fifty Days be kept in mind, so that Ascension does not become an isolated event, but rather a specific witness to the meaning of the Great Fifty

Days as the season of the Spirit. As the narrative of the Apostle's Creed expresses it, "on the third day he rose from the dead, ascended into heaven, and sits at the right hand of God;" and, he sends the Holy Spirit, and "will come to judge the living and the dead." The hymns suitable for this occasion are among the most powerful in *The Book of Hymns* (71-74, 76, 453-58).

XIV.

The Day of Pentecost:
An Order of Worship
with Commentary

GATHERING

Weather permitting, the people may gather outside or in a bright, airy space before the service begins. Here there may be special music and special displays of arts, handcrafts, flowers, and anything representing the gifts which God has given to the congregation. Following the service, this may be a place for gathering and eating.

At the appointed time, the Paschal candle may be brought forward, the people gathered attentively into the opening litany, and everyone may then process into the sanctuary singing the opening hymn.

GREETING AND LITANY OF PRAISE

Our help is in the name of the Lord.
who created heaven and earth.

Sing to God, O kingdoms of the earth;
sing praises to the Lord.
Alleluia!

He rides in the heavens, and sends forth his mighty voice,

Alleluia!

How wonderful is God in his holy places,
  the God of Israel giving strength and power to his
  people!

Alleluia!

All who are led by the Spirit of God are children of God.
Lord, send forth your Spirit,
  and renew the face of the earth. Alleluia!

or
(Sung responsively or recited.)

Antiphon: **Listen! you nations of the world:**
  listen to the word of the Lord.
  Proclaim it from coast to coast,
    declare it to distant islands.

The Lord who scattered Israel will gather his
  people again;
and he will keep watch over them as a
  shepherd watches his flock.

Antiphon: **Listen! you nations of the world:**
  listen to the word of the Lord.
  Proclaim it from coast to coast.
    declare it to distant islands.

With shouts of joy they will come,
  their faces radiantly happy,
for the Lord is so generous to them;
  he showers his people with gifts.

Antiphon: **Listen! you nations of the world:**
  listen to the word of the Lord.
  Proclaim it from coast to coast,
    declare it to distant islands.

243

Young women will dance for joy,
    and men young and old will make merry.
Like a garden refreshed by the rain,
they will never be in want again.
Break into shouts of great joy: Jacob is free
      again!
Teach nations to sing the song: "The Lord
    has saved his people!

Listen! you nations of the world: *(Repeat   refrain.)*

After this the minister says:
    I was glad when they said to me: "Let us go
    into the house of the Lord."

HYMN   Hymn 464, *or see* Book of Hymns *465-67.*

OPENING PRAYER
    The risen Lord is with you.

And also with you.

Let us pray: *A brief pause.*
Almighty God,
    on this day you opened the way of eternal life
    to every race and nation by the promised gift of
    your Holy Spirit:
Shed abroad this gift throughout the world
    by the preaching of the gospel,
    that it may reach to the ends of the earth;
Through Jesus Christ our Lord,
    who lives and reigns with you, in the unity of the Holy
      Spirit,
    for ever and ever. **Amen.**

or

Spirit of the living God,
    visit us again as on the day of Pentecost.

Come, Holy Spirit,

With rushing wind that seeps away all barriers,

Come, Holy Spirit,

With tongues of fire that set our hearts aflame,

Come, Holy Spirit,

With speech that unites the Babel of our tongues,

Come, Holy Spirit,

With love that overleaps the boundaries of race and nation,

Come, Holy Spirit,

With power from above to make our weakness strong,

Come, Holy Spirit,

In the name of Jesus Christ our Lord.   **Amen.**

FIRST LECTION
Joel 2:28-32   (Year A: 1981, 1984, 1987)
Ezekiel 37:1-14   (Year B: 1979, 1982, 1985)
Acts 2:1-21 or Ezekiel 37:1-14
(Acts may be used as the second lection if Ezekiel is used here.)
or
Genesis 11:1-9   (Year C: 1980, 1983, 1986)

PSALM or ANTHEM   Psalm 104:1-4, 24-33 (Years A,B,C)

Antiphon: **Send forth your Spirit, and renew the face of the earth!**

Bless the Lord, O my soul;
  O Lord my God, how excellent is your greatness!
  you are clothed with majesty and splendor.

245

You wrap yourself with light as with a cloak
and spread out the heavens like a curtain.
You lay the beams of your chambers in the
waters above;
you make the clouds your chariot;
you ride on the wings of the wind.
You make the winds your messengers
and flames of fire your servants.

Antiphon: **Send forth your Spirit,
and renew the face of the earth.**
O Lord, how manifold are your works!
in wisdom you have made them all;
the earth is full of your creatures.
Yonder is the great and wide sea
with its living things too many to number,
creatures both small and great.
There move the ships,
and there is that Leviathan,
which you have made for the sport of it.

Antiphon

All creatures look to you
to give them their food in due season.
You give it to them; they gather it;
you open your hand, and they are filled
with good things.
You hide your face, and they are terrified;
you take away their breath,
and they die and return to their dust.

Antiphon

You send forth your Spirit, and they are
created;
and so you renew the face of the earth.
May the glory of the Lord endure for ever;

246

> may the Lord rejoice in all his works.
> He looks at the earth and it trembles;
> > he touches the mountains and they smoke.

Antiphon: **Send forth your Spirit,**
and renew the face of the earth.

SECOND LECTION
Acts 2:1-21   (Years A and C)
I Corinthians   (Year B)
  12:4-13
  or
Acts 1:1-21 *(if not used as first lection)*

HYMN or RESPONSORY
The alternate litany of praise from the opening of the service may be used.

GOSPEL
John 20:19-23   (Year A: 1981, 1984, 1987)
John 16:5-15   (Year B: 1979, 1982, 1985)
John 15:26-27;   (Year C: 1980, 1983, 1986)
  16:4*b*-11

SERMON

RESPONSE TO THE WORD

BAPTISM, CONFIRMATION, AND RENEWAL
Use text as given in the Easter Vigil, or from A Service of Baptism, Confirmation, and Renewal: An Alternate Text, 1976.

PRAYERS OF THE PEOPLE

THE PEACE
Jesus said, "My peace I give to you, not as the world gives."
The peace of the Lord be with you.

And also with you.

Let us exchange signs of reconciliation and peace.

OFFERING
If the Lord's Supper is not celebrated, the service concludes with the following prayers and the final hymn and dismissal and blessing.

PRAYER OF THANKSGIVING
God of wind, word, and fire,
We bless your name this day for sending
    the light and strength of your Holy Spirit;
We give you thanks for all the gifts, great and small,
    which have been poured out upon your children.
Accept us with our gifts to be living praise and witness
    to your love throughout all the earth;
Through Jesus Christ who lives with you in the unity
    of the Holy Spirit, one God, for ever, **Amen.**

LORD'S PRAYER

HYMN

DISMISSAL WITH BLESSING
Go forth in the power of the Holy Spirit!
Proclaim the gospel throughout the earth!
Serve the Lord with gladness, with deeds of justice and
    mercy!

We are sent in the name and power of the Lord!

May the God who raised Jesus from the dead, bless you.

Amen.

May the God to whom our Lord ascended, make his face
shine upon you and be gracious to you.

Amen.

May the Spirit who is the unity of love between
Father and Son, grant you peace forevermore.

Amen. Thanks be to God.

$$\underset{\text{**}}{\text{*}} \qquad \underset{\text{**}}{\text{*}} \qquad \underset{\text{**}}{\text{*}}$$

*If the Lord's Supper is celebrated, the table is prepared
during the singing of the offertory hymn or anthem, and
the gifts brought forward with the offerings.*

GREAT THANKSGIVING

The Lord be with you.

And also with you.

Lift up your hearts.

We lift them to the Lord.

Let us give thanks to the Lord our God.

It is right to give him thanks and praise.

All praise, all thanks are rightly yours, life-giving Lord.
In the beginning your Spirit moved across the face
of the waters,
and when we were formed from the dust of the earth,
you breathed into us the breath of life.
Even when we resisted and grieved you,
your Spirit came upon prophets and teachers,
empowering them to speak your word.
Your steadfast love endures forever.

Therefore we join your people of every time and place,
gathered in word and spirit with the whole company in
heaven and on earth,
singing the never-ending song of praise,

**Holy, holy, holy Lord, God of power and might,
heaven and earth are full of your glory.**

249

Hosanna in the highest.
Blessed is he who comes in the name of the Lord.
Hosanna in the highest!

In the fullness of time, you gave us your Son Jesus Christ,
to be for us the way, the truth, and the life.
At his baptism in the Jordan
your Spirit came upon him and announced him as your
    beloved.
With your Spirit upon him
he turned away the temptations of sin,
proclaimed justice to all peoples,
good news to the poor,
release for the captives,
sight for the blind,
and liberty for the oppressed.
Obedient to your will,
he gave himself in freedom over to death.

On the night he gave himself up for us
he took bread, gave you thanks, broke it,
gave it to his disciples, and said:
"Take, eat, this is my body which is given for you."
When supper was over, he took the cup, gave you
    thanks,
gave it to his disciples, and said:
"Drink from this, all of you;
this is my blood, which seals God's promise,
poured out for you and the many, for the forgiveness of
    sins.
Do this in remembering me."

On the day you raised him from the dead
he was recognized by his disciples
in the breaking of the bread;
In the power of your Holy Spirit

your people have continued day by day
in the breaking of bread and in prayer.

When we eat this bread and drink from this cup
we experience anew the presence of the Lord Jesus
    Christ
and look forward to his coming in final victory.

or

Let us proclaim the mystery of faith:

When we eat this bread and drink this cup,
we proclaim your death, Lord Jesus,
until you come in glory.

Remembering his death and resurrection,
his ascension and promise to be with us always,
we pray that you will send the power of your Holy Spirit
upon us and upon these gifts,
sanctifying this sharing of bread and wine,
that we may share in the body and blood of Christ.
May this sacrifice of praise and thanksgiving,
in union with your Son's sacrifice for us,
be a holy and acceptable offering of ourselves.

Remember, Lord, your church,
Guard it from all evil, and preserve it by your love.
Gather it together from the four winds into your
    kingdom.
By the baptism of water and your Holy Spirit
send us as your witnesses into all the world,
in the name of Jesus Christ our Lord.

Through him, with him, and in him,
in the unity of the Holy Spirit,
all glory and honor is yours, Almighty God,
now and for ever. Come, Lord Jesus!

As Jesus has taught us, we are bold to pray:

LORD'S PRAYER   **Our Father . . .**   *All pray together.*

BREAKING OF THE BREAD

GIVING OF BREAD AND THE CUP

PRAYER AFTER COMMUNION

HYMN or DOXOLOGICAL STANZA

DISMISSAL WITH BLESSING
Go forth into the world, rejoicing in the power
of the Holy Spirit!

Thanks be to God, Alleluia!

The blessing of Almighty God,
Father, Son, and Holy Spirit, be with you
this day and for ever.

Amen! Alleluia!

Commentary

This is the great climax of the Easter-Pentecost Season. On this day we remember and celebrate the fullness of God's promises in Jesus Christ. Before us this day is the whole sweep of Christ's death and resurrection, his ascension, and the sending of the Holy Spirit with all God's gifts and commissioning power for our ministries. This great occasion should be marked with special gatherings and a festive common meal. It is especially fitting to celebrate the Lord's Supper with great joy.

The music should be glorious and may include Easter as well as Pentecost texts. If there is to be a gathering outside the church building, instrumental music is appropriate. We may draw, for example, upon the French medieval and

Moravian traditions in having brass fanfare and/or chorales, perhaps from a church tower or other high place. There may be a festival or display of the "varieties of gifts" given to the church: images of its various ministries and missions, its common life, the arts, and its hopes and expectations. This should be an occasion of freedom, sharing, and hospitality among all. This in itself is a sign and a witness to the "Spirit which has been poured out into our hearts."

If a procession is formed behind the Paschal candle, the choir may wish to sing the canticle found in Contemporary Worship Series, No. 5: *Services of the Word*, published by the Inter-Lutheran Commission on Worship, (Augsburg, 1972), pp. 68-79. The refrain may be introduced first, and the congregation responds as they move toward and enter the church. Or, if the space is relatively short, Wesley's great hymn, "See How Great a Flame Aspires" (464), is especially appropriate. If this hymn is not already known, it may be learned by the congregation for this service. The opening sentence is used only if a procession is to follow.

The congregation may return to the same fellowship room or outdoor space for a fellowship meal following the service. Festivities and arts displays may last on into the afternoon.

This day presents several opportunities for responses to the Word. There may be musical responses or a period of witness and testimony to the faith—particularly to the service ministries of the local and global church in which the Holy Spirit is at work. A creed may be used by the entire congregation, or there may be a period of free prayer.

This day also is a most suitable time for Baptisms, Confirmations, and Renewal of the Baptismal covenant. If the baptismal Renewal has not been celebrated on Easter Sunday, it is strongly urged that *A Service of Baptism, Confirmation, and Renewal: An Alternate Text, 1976,* or its appropriate sections, be used as the main response to the Word. This should be given ample time to unfold with power, and not be rushed or merely sandwiched in. This may require shortening the sermon slightly. Again, the proclamatory power of the sacrament speaks for itself, if done well and prayerfully. Careful preparations must be made, and particular attention given to the instructions leading to baptismal Renewal or Confirmation. Those being prepared should have a clear appreciation for the rite which takes place in the context of the Pentecost Gospel and the whole congregational service.

Another possibility for the service, or perhaps for the presentation at a common meal, is a drama based upon the disciples' experience on the first Pentecost. In particular, people may experience the contrast between Babel (texts read simultaneously in several languages) and the unity of utterance in the preaching of the gospel. The Scripture lections suggest various possible media presentations as well: the valley of dry bones, the wind and fire, water and the Spirit—all these may be presented along with nonbiblical or contemporary readings as interpretations. Babel and Pentecost provide rich and inexhaustible themes.

The celebration of the Lord's Supper should be permeated with joy. Hymns 318, 466, and 467 are particularly suitable.

Notes

1. For further clarification of this term and a summary of the history of early celebrations of the Pascha (Passover-Easter), see *Seasons of the Gospel*, pp. 17-21.
2. *From Ashes to Easter* is obtainable from The Liturgical Conferences, 810 Rhode Island Avenue NE, Washington, D.C. 20018.
3. The Easter Triduum (literally "three days") is the Latin name given to the span of time from the celebration of Maundy Thursday sunset up to the sunset of Easter Day. If we adopt the biblical reckoning of days, beginning with sunset and ending at the next sunset, we find that three days include the events of the Last Supper, the arrest and trial, the crucifixion, burial, and the resurrection "on the first day of the week"—that is, on Sunday following the Jewish Sabbath. The intention is theological and liturgical integrity rather than temporal accuracy.
4. See *Seasons of the Gospel*, pp. 19-20.
5. The Great Fifty Days takes it name from the period of time, reckoned from the book of Acts, between the resurrection and the receiving of the Holy Spirit by the whole church at Jerusalem. Forty days is the symbolic number, inherited also from the Old Testament, of days which marked Jesus' post-resurrection appearances until his ascension. The Fifty Days also echoes the ancient Hebrew celebration of Pentecost as well.
6. *The Grail/Gelineau Psalter* (Chicago: G.I.A. Publications, Inc., 1974); Deiss, Lucien, C.C.Sp., *Biblical Hymns and Psalms*, 2 vols.

(Cincinnati: World Library Publications, Inc., 1965, 1971); *Daily Prayer of the Church*, in Contemporary Worship Series (no. 9), published by the Inter-Lutheran Commission on Worship (Minneapolis: Augsburg Publishing House, 1977), pp. 68-69.

7. From the beginning of their written form, each of the four Gospels contained the passion as a continuous narrative. These narratives are quite different in form from the rest of the materials in the Gospels that were handed down in various collections of oral traditions. The center point of the gospel accounts is preserved in the church's proclamatory reading of these narratives in their fullness.

8. A booklet containing the full text with introduction and extensive documentation for further study may be obtained from the National Conference of Christians and Jews, 43 West 75th Street, New York, N.Y. 10019; or from any of their regional offices in metropolitan areas.

9. Saint Basil of Caesarea, *Baptismal Homilies*, in Edward Yarnold's *The Awe-Inspiring Rites of Initiation; Baptismal Homilies of the Fourth Century* (London: St. Paul's Publications, 1971).

10. "A Common Eucharistic Prayer" is an ecumenical prayer based upon several sources, most notably the ancient Alexandrian anaphora of Saint Basil of Caesarea, and the Latin original of Eucharistic Prayer IV of the *Roman Sacramentary*. It was first published by a committee composed of Roman Catholics, Episcopalians, Lutherans, Presbyterians, and United Methodists in 1975, and subsequently was authorized as an alternative eucharistic prayer for Rite II of the *Authorized Services* in the Episcopal Church.

11. This Introduction, Order of Seder Service, and Commentary are taken from *The Living Heritage of Passover*, with minor adaptations. A booklet, along with other interpretative materials, may be purchased from the Anti-Defamation League of B'Nai B'Rith, 315 Lexington Avenue, New York, N.Y. 10016.

12. Cited in *The Liturgical Year*, by Adrian Nocent, O.S.B., translated by M. J. O'Connell (Collegeville, Minn.: The Liturgical Press, 1977), Vol. III, pp. 235-36. The whole four-volume set is an excellent resource for serious study of the Christian year. Though based on the Roman Catholic version of the three-year lectionary, it provides valuable theological and homiletical insights for anyone using the new ecumenical lectionary upon which *Word and Table, Seasons of the Gospel,* and *From Ashes to Fire* are based.